# New Faith

"Readers may be surprised by Sheron Patterson's candor or even disagree with her diagnoses, but they will appreciate her passionate and pastoral attempt to address the suffering that Black women endure in the name of love and faith."

—Renita J. Weems
Vanderbilt Divinity School

"Sheron Patterson's work is full of vitality and power. This volume challenges not only African American women but also the church itself and the field of pastoral theology to look at suffering in new ways—with an eye toward tangible empowerment of the oppressed."

—Patricia H. Davis
Perkins School of Theology

# New Faith

A Black Christian Woman's Guide to Reformation,
Re-Creation, Rediscovery, Renaissance,
Resurrection, and Revival

Sheron C. Patterson

Fortress Press
Minneapolis

Cover art: Howardena Pindell, *Autobiography: Water/Ancestors, Middle Passage/Family Ghosts* (1989), Wadsworth Atheneum, Hartford, Connecticut, The Ella Gallup Sumner and Mary Catlin Sumner Collection Fund. Used by permission.
Interior design: Beth Wright

Unless otherwise noted, Scripture quotations are from the Revised Standard Version of the Bible, copyright © 1946, 1952, 1971 by the Division of Christian Education of the National Council of the Churches of Christ in the U.S.A., and are used by permission.
Scripture quotations from the New American Standard Bible (NAS), copyright © 1960, 1962, 1963, 1968, 1971, 1972, 1973, 1975, 1977 by the Lockman Foundation, are used by permission.
Scripture quotations from the New Revised Standard Version Bible (NRSV), copyright © 1989 by the Division of Christian Education of the National Council of the Churches of Christ in the USA, are used by permission.

Library of Congress
Patterson, Sheron C.
    New faith: a black Christian woman's guide to reformation, recreation, rediscovery, renaissance, resurrection, and revival / Sheron C. Patterson.
        p.    cm.
    Includes bibliographical references.
    ISBN 0-8006-3158-7 (alk. paper)
    1. Black theology. 2. Afro-American women—Religious life.
    I. Title.
BT 82.7 .P38 2000
248.8'43'08996073—dc21

                                                    00-035466

The paper used in this publication meets the minimum requirements of American National Standard for Information Sciences — Permanence of Paper for Printed Library Materials, ANSI Z329.48-1984.

Manufactured in the U.S.A.                          AF1-3158
04    03    02    01    00    2    3    4    5    6    7    8    9    10    11

# Contents

# Preface

*to the sisters sitting in the pews*

**Black Christian sisters,** you've been silent far too long. It's time to ask the difficult questions about church, the Bible, and even Jesus Christ. You've been still far too long. It's time to press, pull, tug at all you've been taught about faith to see if it's really true. You've been theologically naive far too long. It's time to read for yourselves, interpret for yourselves, and think for yourselves about God. We've listened to what Anglo theologians have said and to what Black male theologians have said. Now it's our turn. And you know, nobody can say it like us!

New Faith is the key that unlocks all that women should have known a long time ago about ourselves and what God is saying to us. Yes, God speaks to women powerfully and profoundly. New Faith will give you the courage to listen to what God is saying to you, too. I wrote this book because God spoke to me regarding the oppression of church women. God saw the depression, despair, and downheartedness in us despite our Sunday best. God saw the way church women lost their natural minds just to have a man, and God declared it was time for something new: a New Faith! A new way of understanding and relating to the same faithful, flawless God who has been our bridge over troubled water and our rock in the weary land.

New Faith streams forward nonstop. The more information one gathers, the further on she must move. Each chapter will propel you ahead as you meditate on God's love for you, your love for self, your love for your sisters, and finally your love for your brothers. We deserve to move ahead, and we are taking our churches, families, and community with us. If we don't get ourselves up out of this mess, who will?

I wish to thank my doctoral studies advisor, Dr. Patricia Davis, and my doctoral thesis supervisor, Dr. Barbara Cambridge. The unwavering confidence of these two scholars carried me when I was faltering. I thank Perkins School of Theology at Southern Methodist University for a doctoral program that permitted me to tell the truth my way.

I say thank you to the brave sisters who participated in the doctoral focus group. Their honesty and candor propelled this book into being. I thank the Jubilee United Methodist Church family for always accepting me, an innovative, provocative, high-strung preacher, as their pastor. Even when they did not understand me, they loved me.

I thank my parents William and Johnsie Covington, who reared me in the Christian church, taught me the Word of God, and lived before me lives of love and commitment.

I thank my awesome husband, Robert, who honors what God is doing in my life by enabling me to do it. He cares for me and about me ceaselessly. Our sons, Robert Jr. and Christian, helped their mom during this writing season by giving me hugs and kisses while I wrote.

Last, and most of all, I thank the Lord for creating a girl with eyes to see, ears to hear, a mind to understand, and hands to write. God pours into me a fearlessness that spills into my writing. Some think I am naturally brave. Oh, no: "The Lord is my light and my salvation; whom shall I fear? The Lord is the defense of my life; of whom shall I be afraid?"

# 1. Counter-Cultural Strut

"Walk while you have light, that the darkness may not overtake you." (John 12:35 NAS)

**Girlfriend,** as Black, Christian, and female, you are awesome times three. But to blossom into the true diva that you are, you can't just go with the flow. Stop going along to get along. If you know it's not right, don't accept it. Move against the grain, counter the culture. Your authentic beauty won't shine through acquiescence.

That's what I discovered the hard way. It began when I could not take being treated as "just a woman" anymore. You know the treatment: being looked down on, being looked over for promotions, being ignored, and being expected less of. I'd gone along to get along for over thirty-five years, until I realized that I was in pain. Being a Black Christian woman in a sexist, racist world hurts. But there is no one to tell. I turned my gaze from what was and looked at what ought to be and the rest of my body followed. I started moving in a direction that countered the rest of the world. To continue on with the ways of this world would betray my own being. "I" became important. My self gained value. It could be silenced and ignored for the so-called common good no more.

I hadn't planned to leave the flow permanently, but merely to pull over to the shoulder of the road to sort some things out. When I pulled over to search for the sources of the pain, I realized that some things were not adding up and that I was tired of pretending they did. My questions included: Why were most of my beautiful, degreed, and well-paid girlfriends unable to find men for committed relationships? Why is the first word out of the mouths of many brothers regarding relationships with sisters *submit*? (Especially when they themselves are neither biblically literate or involved in a relationship with the Lord.) And why is it that on Sunday mornings Black churches are filled with women, but these same women refuse to be led by one of their own?

When I pulled over to the shoulder of the road to search for the sources of the pain, I saw my beloved Black community differently. My familiar land was a strange place where the sisters were the second-class citizens and were taught by their faith to enjoy it. It was a place where they loved them some Jesus, but believed Jesus' promises for others, not themselves. Church was a focal point that kept them full of "Amens" but in a plantation-like existence.

## Predestined to Be the Same

In sociology books, Black women are depicted as strong matriarchs who can raise a houseful of children, hold down two jobs, and run a hair salon out of the back bedroom on Saturday mornings. But when it comes to their men, they become weak. That dichotomy—strong in the world, weak with men—troubled me, because I realized I had been predestined to be the same. The only difference was that I stopped to think about it while the others kept on accepting.

I thought about receiving Barbie dolls with extensive wardrobes that consumed hours of time in dressing and undressing for parties and trips. I remember baby dolls that I was supposed to want to cradle and caress and pretend they were real. I was also expected to pretend to be a real mother and practice being responsible. All the while I was cuddling plastic babies and coordinating their wardrobes, the boys my age were receiving doctor's kits, chemistry sets, or toy firemen's gear to equip them for careers.

I thought about the piano, dance, and French lessons that I went to in the afternoons after school. All this was done to ensure that I'd be cultured and prepared. The neighborhood boys were outside playing, and I wondered, if they weren't being prepared, why were we?

Influences such as these shuttled me through a programmed girlhood into a planned womanhood. A generational noose was waiting for me to grow up into it. These influences seemed so right, so Black, so hip, because everybody was on board and in agreement with them. It's just the way things were—no questions asked.

These influences governed my development like training wheels on a kid's bike to keep me on the path with the others. They defined what it meant to be a girl child in the Black Christian community. These influences had power over me, despite the love and nurture I received daily from my parents. Mom and Dad told me that I was good, smart, pretty, and capable of doing anything. Although I believed them on one level, the influences said otherwise, and they had more power than my parents.

Television was another influence. My favorite program was *Soul Train*. Long before music videos were available, *Soul Train* was the only place to catch performances of popular music artists. *Soul Train* not only exposed me to images of my favorite singers, but it subconsciously sculpted my understanding of the place and role of women. Quietly, with little fanfare, the program's cameramen incrementally molded my thought processes, rationales, and concepts of how things ought to be for women. Their repetitious, extreme close-up angles on dancing women clad in blouses with plunging necklines, tight hot pants, or micro-miniskirts told me that these dancers were more important and noticeable than the women who chose to cover their flesh. I learned that women were important based on what they wore and how what they wore made men feel.

Music was also an influence. As an only child, I wanted companionship (not sleep) at nighttime. But music was the only friend I could find during those sleepless nights. So I usually curled up beside the radio and lived inside the world of lyrics and what they must have meant to the composer. "I'm Going to Make You Love Me" is the first song that I consciously remember. My older girl cousins sang it just as if they were singing a spiritual in church. Their conviction convinced me that whoever "he" was, it was my job to make him mine, whether he wanted to be or not. I soon grew to understand that music taught women and men how to relate to each other. The lyrics directed the way I should feel. If it was on the radio, I thought, it had to be right.

Popular films were significant influences on my adolescence. "Blaxploitation" films à la *Shaft*, *Superfly*, and *Coffey* peaked in popularity in the mid-1970s, just at the time I looked old enough to sneak into theaters and see what the R-rated movies were all about. This genre of cinema was characterized by brazen, bold brothers with big 'fros, blasting guns, and furious fists who decided they must right any wrong they could find. They'd fight and cuss up a storm, all the while styling and profiling. Women in these films were accessories in the exciting lives of the men. Such films taught me that women are at their best when they are on a man's arm or in his bed. I wanted excitement, so I decided to find a man whose life I could watch and accessorize.

Church synthesized all influences and made sense of them. I've been in church all my life. I trusted it blindly. I believed that church was the place to process all information and try to make sense out of what was happening. God was known to perform miracles and wonders. "Lord," I prayed, "help me make some sense out of this mess."

Sunday school lessons taught me that God was a man. The parts of the Bible that I'd heard spoke of God blessing or rescuing or leading men. Therefore, in my young opinion, church was a large group, primarily women, listening to a man talk about another big man with rules for the lesser men. Since there were few men around, I assumed the women were stand-ins for the men. They were runners-up in the contest of faith: they were close enough to the core of importance to sense the power but not own it. They could not feel the fire; they could only glimpse the flame.

One Sunday morning, as we stood up to sing yet another hymn about the big man and the little men ("Rise Up, O Men of God"), it all became clear to me. Even though we women weren't men, we *should* have been. Then those hymns would be about us. But since we weren't men, we women had a job to do. We had to:

1. Accessorize the lives of men.
2. Get the attention of men using our clothing.
3. Make men love us.

From that point on, everything I saw and heard made sense. The Bible presented women in minor roles. Often they weren't even important enough for names. This explained the carefully slotted spaces that they held in the society around me. Now I understood why there weren't any women standing beside Dr. Martin Luther King Jr. in the photos I saw of the great March on Washington. Why should there be? Women were probably somewhere working on the three goals like the rest of us. There were no women preachers, few women in political office, and few women leaders in my community. Other women, I assumed, were busy on the same task that I was. The church made sense of other issues, too. For example, the church made Black men precious. They were the closest thing we had to the big man. The few of them that were around were valued and catered to. Close proximity to one of them was a blessing.

## Becoming Somebody

I received my first blessing at the age of thirteen when I secured my first "real" boyfriend in junior high school. I became Somebody in the eyes of God. The fact that James was two years my senior made me more important. He didn't have much to offer in terms of looks, personality, or a future, but I was happy just because I had him.

This boyfriend was a watershed event, because years earlier I had decided not to wear makeup until I had a boyfriend. I believed I wasn't worth beautifying until then. With James in tow, I had a reason to purchase fruity, sticky lip glosses and metallic eyeshadows at Woolworth's department store. He was my license to live.

I wasn't old enough to date him, but we sure could talk on the phone late at night when my parents were asleep. We'd talk so long that my ear would go numb from the receiver. I didn't care; a boyfriend was the ultimate activity for me. Sometimes during our conversations I would hear yelling and screaming in the background at James's house. I eventually learned that the screamers were his parents engaged in one of their regular fights. This never meant much to me; I was focused on James. He appeared unaffected by it. But as our relationship deepened, he would become hostile if I disagreed with him. His dogmatic nature escalated into threats of violence and bodily harm. I assumed he was joking. "Who would get so mad and promise to hit me over a minor point?" I thought. When I laughed off his threats, he became even madder.

On one of our rare dates, he secretly came to my neighborhood, and we walked around the streets together. His temper flared in the midst of our conversation. Again, I laughed. This time there was no telephone receiver to buffer the blows. He slapped me. I stopped laughing and disagreeing with him. I kept on talking with him by phone. At the time I did not see myself as a battering victim. But I wondered if God wanted me to be slapped. And I wondered if the slap was a part of what it meant to be in a relationship with a man. Eventually we drifted apart. I went on to other boys, who would make me Somebody again.

In senior high school, I longed to hang out with the cool girls. They were the ones who smoked cigarettes in the restrooms and reefer in the parking lot. They wore tight, short clothing and were masters of every profane word I'd ever heard. The cool girls were also sexually active and proud of it. Their pride led them to give impromptu sex lectures in the hallways to those of us who they knew had no chance of living cool like them.

Naturally the cool girls had cool boyfriends. These were boys who wore shades outdoors and indoors, boys who cut class, stayed high, and didn't care. These boys had the hippest clothes—high platform shoes, elephant bell-bottom jeans, and big, fluffy 'fros that swayed elegantly when they swaggered by. The boring guys were polite, conscientious about schoolwork, and spoke proper English. I wanted a cool guy.

Momma and Dad wouldn't let me be a cool girl. They wouldn't let me dress like the cool girls, and they would have killed me if I acted like them. Therefore the cool boys were out of reach. I was confused. Wasn't I supposed to seek a boyfriend? Which way should I go? Why couldn't I meet the requirements to get the boys I wanted?

Attending college was like being caught up in a frenzied antelope herd. The propulsion of thousands carried me in a direction I did not choose. It was as though I had joined a team sport with other beautiful, smart young women. The goal was to lose your self-respect and gain a man. In the herd, I first felt the intense heat of competing for a man: straining to catch an eye, laboring for his favor. I first felt the raw pangs of recklessness to accept a piece of a man even though he may have belonged to another woman. I experienced the highs and lows of being chosen or being dumped. The clamor to have a boyfriend spread like a common disease. Every one of us had it bad.

## Walking Counter-Culture

In the midst of this madness, I heard God calling me into the ordained ministry. This call was contrary to the direction of the herd. It was amazing that God spoke loud enough to be heard above the frenzied dating din. For at least nine months I felt God tugging at my heart to reroute my gifts away from the materialism of most Buppies and toward a life of service. God's invitation became crystal clear in January 1981, exactly four months before I was to graduate. Immediately, I scrapped plans for film school and scrambled to find a seminary—any seminary would do. I just had to get close to God. I knew there was true Somebodiness there.

Completing the application for seminary was easy. Explaining to friends, classmates, and my parents why I was going was the hard part. They knew no female ministers. "What are you heading toward?" they asked. "How can you go somewhere no one else has gone before?" they whispered. Their doubts gave me doubt. Their lack of faith tried to extinguish the flame God had started in my soul. But I entered seminary anyway. Little did I know that I was beginning to walk counter-culture.

The one-two punch of racism and sexism greeted me the first week of seminary. In the seminary's liberal Christian environment, these two "isms" were not overbearing. They were polite and gentle. The Whites ignored me, and the Black men, though cordial, thought little of me or of my abilities to pastor. Cloistered in middle-class Black America, I was naive; my parents successfully shielded me from White people's wrath. Sexism was not even in my vocabulary: never did it occur to me that men would denigrate me on the basis of my gender.

Adding to this vacuum of support was the weighty reality that there was one other Black woman in the seminary. Instead of being sisters, we were like two isolated islands in the sea. I had no women to call and ask for help. Most of my battles I fought alone. If I won, I celebrated alone. If I lost, I cried alone. Isolation was a way of life. Aloneness and by-myselfness was my norm.

Life after seminary was like moving from the frying pan and into the fire. Isolation increased as a pastor. The sexism did not come from men, who basically left me alone. It was women who besieged me and let me know that they preferred a clergyman. The young women, whom I had envisioned rallying around me, left in droves for churches led by male pastors. Many of the women who stayed were distant and cold. They did not know what to do with me. Was I their daughter, friend, or foe? Showing their disappointment that I was not a man, as I should have been, they just sat there and watched me.

I began to observe the women of my flock. I saw the effects on their lives of male-dominated biblical language and male images of God. They did not see themselves as worthy of self-love or anyone else's love. I saw their faith in everybody else but themselves. I saw them suffering in relationships with the men in their lives. I saw the lack of unity among them, how they hated each other and themselves. I became angry not with them but with the institution that miseducated them. The church has been not their helper but their hindrance. I asked the question, "Am I the only one to see this?"

## Birthing New Faith

Determined to find out if I'd really seen anything, I decided to return to seminary for doctoral study. A Ph.D. in why sisters let the brothers drive them crazy?! "That would never work," some said to me. I pressed on anyway. I needed a way to cope with the reasons for my anger. The unofficial reason for the doctorate was to get to the bottom of this mess and to ensure that I was not crazy. For the official record, I needed to validate all that I had seen and felt as universal for Black Christian women. Maybe the suffering of sisters inflicted by the church could be remedied if someone proved it, wrote it down. My method was to gather twelve Black Christian women into a reading group for eight weeks. I wanted to know if they felt the pain I had felt. I needed to hear their perceptions of their world. I wondered how the influences of growing up female, Black, and Christian had had an impact on their lives.

The sisters were as diverse as sisters can be: thin and overweight, light-skinned and dark-skinned, college degrees and GEDs, married and single, twenties and forties, United Methodists, nondenominational, and Baptists. Their common element was that they had experienced God and Black men and wanted to learn if there was a connection.

What a time we had! Our literary guides were the Holy Bible and Terry McMillan's *Waiting to Exhale*. We explored the Scriptures from the perspective of 1990s Black women with attitudes about everything. We dared to utter contradictions and critiques. Previously, this had been the privilege of dead European male theologians. This time the sisters sat around and discussed their interpretations of what God had done back then and was doing now.

McMillan's frankness opened up channels of honesty within the women, and testimonies of affairs, lost loves, abuse, good men, and bad men flowed like rivers. Her novel helped the women to understand the connection between the way they see God and the way they relate to men. The more they talked about McMillan's characters—Bernadine, Savannah, Robin, and Gloria—the clearer the connection became.

Even though *Waiting to Exhale* greased the wheels of dialogue and self-expression, there were still obstacles to understanding and growth facing the women. Fear was a primary issue. Anytime women intentionally come together for self-improvement, others become nervous. Anxiety-ridden husbands paraded back and forth outside our conference-room locale sometimes, bellowing their pleas to know what was going on. The women feared investing time to study themselves. It was not seen as appropriate to spend so much time on self rather than family. They feared critiquing men—it simply was not done. Their fear said, "It is not wise to hold Black men accountable. Male leadership is never to be challenged."

Miseducation was an obstacle. They were taught to give much of their power away. They shared the "musts" that their mothers taught them. But those hand-me-down "musts" were really a bunch of sexist myths. Apathy was an obstacle. They were unable to make major changes in their lives because they saw no real reason to. If other women were suffering, it was too bad.

This group of brave sisters concretized four beliefs about Black Christian women.

1. Black women receive a Christian miseducation from the sexist historic Black Christian church. This miseducation prevents them from seeing the danger of ecclesial apartheid (minority rule) and keeps them blindly loyal to pastors and churches that do more harm than good.

2. Black Christian women are taught to accept domination from men for Christ's sake. The miseducation is most clearly seen in their relationships with the men in their lives. They have misappropriated suffering for

Christ's sake with suffering for the sake of their men. I call this "unnecessary suffering."

3. Most of them have never heard of womanism, but they would be better off because of it. Black women need the strength and broad interpretation offered by Black female theologian sisters.

4. Clergy women and lay women need each other, but they are trained by sexism to hate each other, to compete with each other, and to resist female leadership.

Now you understand why I had to call an end to the madness. This history is harmful. That's why I started moving counter-culture. I've grown to appreciate my position, but I'd like to have some sisters with me. Together we can create something new. Fortified by our shared dilemma, we must move together. We must move with swiftness against the grain. If we strike out together, we can redirect and reshape ourselves.

Let's rebuild ourselves. We Black church women by nature are builders. We can tirelessly (and often quite stylishly) commit our hat-wearing, cobbler-baking selves to a task and toil relentlessly until it is complete. That's why the Black church exists today. Your great-grandmother and mine fried chicken and baked pies for the building fund. Your great-aunt and mine were immovable members of tiny churches, placing the few copper coins they owned in the collection plates. They prayed those ancient chants rhythmically, putting rappers to shame ("O we thank you God that our covers were not our winding sheets. . . ."). They mumbled and moaned to the beat of celestial drums. They churched the Black religious community into being.

Yet even though they built it, their church does not reflect their faces, their womanness. There is no resemblance between this offspring and its mother. Black women keep on feeding it with their time, their talents, and their tithes, but they have been mauled by the being they gave birth to. The shame is not the mauling. The shame is that the creature is still being fed, loved, and nurtured, despite the pain.

Our great-grands did the best they could. Now it is our turn. We can do better. We can contribute to the Black church in new ways, in Black women's way. There is room for male *and* female leadership in the church.

We must have something new—a New Faith for living these days as Black Christian women. Let's start from the very beginning and go through the Bible again. Let's hear wisdom from the mouths of *women* and men.

New Faith gives us the chance to start from scratch, set our goals, name our God in our language, speak our faith in our terms. To do all of this, we must move counter-culture. Let's move. Let's strut. We must strut. We can't crawl—that's for babies. We can't walk—this is the twenty-first century. Walking is an ancient mode of operation. Therefore, we strut. We take our time but keep moving. We strut. Placing one foot in front of the other, we keep moving. Swing those arms. Lean back. Tilt the head, cock the chin, sweep the butt. Strut to the rhythm of some finger-popping Christian tune. Focus on the music. Focus on your steps. Focus on your God and the power that God gives you.

And let us strut toward what we can be in the name of Jesus Christ.

## Reflection Questions

1. What would make you walk counter-culture?
2. What didn't "add up" in your childhood?
3. Do you engage in unnecessary suffering?
4. Have you been miseducated?

# 2. What Is New Faith?

"... and put on the new self, which in the likeness of God has been created in righteousness and holiness of the truth." (Eph. 5:24 NAS)

**New Faith** is for and about Black women. It was born out of an interpretation of Scriptures that leads sisters to healing and wholeness. It's called "new" because it rejects the male domination, female subjugation, and hierarchy of the genders found in the prevailing interpretations of Scripture. Yet it retains "faith," the loyal embrace of Jesus Christ as Lord, God as the creator, and the Holy Spirit as the sustainer. When we adopt New Faith, it is akin to putting on the new self. You will discover a new likeness of the same God.

New Faith benefits us all. It benefits some of us like a flashlight in a darkened room. When Kim telephoned me late one night, she was spiritually dazed and biblically confused. She was no Christian rookie. Kim had been planted in the pews of church since birth. But now, after a few months of comprehensive Bible study, this woman discovered that she was tired of being just a girl in God's house. The in-depth studies opened the door to her spiritual maturity. She was introduced to Esther, Ruth, Deborah, and other strong women of the Bible. Kim's pain surfaced when she realized that her pastor had never mentioned any of these women in his sermons. Her husband, the chief deacon, had never mentioned them in their family devotions either. It was as though women did not exist in the Bible. Kim felt betrayed. She called me to express her uneasiness. She was embarrassed to be uneasy with her pastor and husband's deficits and her own discovery. But her uneasiness signaled what happens to us when we discover that there is more to God than the people in our lives have told us. Kim is a prime candidate for New Faith.

New Faith benefits women like a shelter when they are caught in a rainstorm. Tina is a casual Christian. Raised with a lukewarm church affiliation, she never understood the Bible, but she respectfully listened to others who did. Tina lived with Archie for nine years. She prayed every day of those years that he would marry her. Archie always produced an excuse—lack of money, the need to finish a college degree, or simply that the timing was off. Finally he found a rock-solid excuse: Tina was infertile. Archie said, "I'll never marry a woman who cannot give me kids!" After rounds at fertility clinics, Tina heard a voice speaking clearly to her pitiful predicament: "Get out."

"I knew it was God," Tina said. "I did not know much about God, but I felt in my gut that I was being guided and directed out of a life of constant chaos." Tina is a candidate for New Faith as she rebuilds her life.

Are you a candidate for New Faith? Are you tired of a partial understanding? Are you tired of just hearing about God, never knowing God for yourself? Are you eager for scriptural interpretation for the twenty-first century? Then you are ready for New Faith.

## The Goal of New Faith

The goal of New Faith is to bring restoration to damaged souls of Black women so they may see God clearly, themselves royally, other women as their sisters, and men as their brothers. If you have been bruised, bumped, and bullied by the "isms," you need New Faith. The sexism on your job, the classism you face at the mall, the racism everywhere, and even the ageism that will someday greet you are real and fierce. The damage inflicted has inhibited your ability to relate with others as God would have you.

New Faith equips women to initiate and sustain right relationships by giving primacy to healthy relationships—not those ailing ones that keep us up crying all night, or those that force us to be treated as though we were dirt. There is a four-step plan. New Faith addresses your relationship first with God, then with yourself, with your sisters, and then with your men.

First, New Faith puts you and God on a first-name basis. We begin with God because God is our genesis. We possess powerful memories of where and how we first met God. Hold tight to those memories; they will be the sustenance for our journey. Our faithful embrace of what is good about God encourages us to revel in God's glory. Let's put on our shouting shoes. Yes, we know God set free those Hebrew slaves and showed Pharaoh who was boss. God is a liberator. Yes, God is our shepherd who leads us by the still waters, and we don't have to want for anything! God is our provider.

And where did you meet God? Was it in Sunday school? Or visiting grandma's house? Was it a coworker's invitation? Or did you meet God when you walked quietly by the river after a traumatic event in your life? Wherever it was and whenever it was, meeting God was the best thing you could have done. This is the most important relationship of your life.

However, sisters, we do have baggage in our relationships with God. Baggage is the stuff that we don't need to carry around, but we do because a negative event in our lives won't allow us to release the bag. Some misguided saint heaped a sick belief system upon us. Or the actions of others have soured us on God. And as a result, some of us experience God as the parent who deserted us, or the guardian who is too strict, or the provider who never loved us the way we loved them.

Catherine and her sisters grew up in a home where church was the main event. They praised God with great fervor on Sunday mornings but were raped by their father the other six days of the week.

"I know all about the God of Sunday mornings," Catherine said. "The goodness, the joy, and all. But I know nothing about the God of the rest of the week. There was no such God for me when I was at home. I thought that God only lived at church."

New Faith meets Catherine in her abused soul with restoring, woman-centered hope. Her painful past won't allow her to reach out using the traditional way. New Faith offers a fresh route and an uncontaminated face to the same God by translating her pain into a pathway of healing.

## Fall in Love with You

Second, New Faith helps you examine your relationship with yourself. New Faith wants you to fall in love with you. It is time for you to concentrate on who you are in Jesus. You are something good. You are worthy. You are a vessel of the Holy Spirit. You are rich in God's grace. Black women go through so many needless changes about loving themselves. There is the unspoken Black-church-lady law that mandates us to prove our authentic Christianity by forgetting ourselves and loving others. We become selfless caretakers of the world. But someone forgot to mention the fact that if you can't love yourself, it is impossible to love others.

Yes, we go through changes. We receive mixed messages about whether or not we are good enough to love.

The American standard of beauty makes our skin too dark, our noses too wide, our hair too nappy, and, most of all, our butts too big to be considered beautiful. Concentrating on self has been hard for us because it has been painful. Allow New Faith to lead you in this sacred act of abundant introspection. You can lavish yourself. This is a form of worshipping God. We are temples of the Holy Spirit. Have you been there to worship yet? Praise God for your arms, legs, face, and teeth. Lift up hallelujahs for the breath that flows out of your lungs. Shout gratitude for the potential inside you to do all things in God's name. Go to the temple and have your own prayer and praise service every day.

Third, New Faith allows us to examine the ways we relate to one another as women. New Faith puts the "sister" back in *sister*. Do you remember the childhood bliss of huddling with other girls in the hallways of school, jumping around with no cares in the world? In that cocoon of girls, you could be who you were. There was no fear of betrayal, being out-dressed, or having your man taken away. That's what being sisters is all about.

The truth is that we call each other sisters but act more like adversaries. Division dilutes our power as Christian women in our churches. We don't need competition; that's not God's plan for women. We need comrades. New Faith appeals for unity, an important force in the midst of strife. When we look closer, we see that our disdain for other women stems from our training that teaches us to devalue each other. Little daily incidents teach us this lesson, such as seeing no women in the pulpit, seeing few women in leadership positions, rarely hearing sermons about women as heroines. We've been trained to see ourselves as "less than." The church has groomed us to carry a mild distaste for other women.

If women do not see themselves in leadership positions, they subconsciously assume that they should not and cannot lead. It is believed that men have the power and that the role of women, as women have witnessed it, is powerlessness. Therefore, group meetings in which power can be coalesced are shunned. For example, Sheila admitted that she did not enjoy participating in women's ministries at her church. "It's just a bunch of women. I can't stand being in a room full of them. They can never get anything accomplished. They talk too much, and they aren't about anything. I've got better things to do with my time," she said. The bold truth is that gender does matter. And with the same tenacity that Black people have declared racism a sin, we New Faith women must declare sexism the equal sin. Gender matters color our world and slant the playing field. "Gender distortions may even contaminate the positive lived experiences that teach people most intensely and persuasively about God. A woman convinced of her second-class citizenship can easily find herself in worship seeking crumbs from the masters' table."[1]

New Faith is for women of all economic classes and education levels. Classism is not acceptable for New Faith. This is not a rich woman's faith or a ghetto belief system. It is a faith for us all. Statistics tell us that the majority of Black women live at or below the poverty level. I believe that "the daily struggles for poor Black women must serve as a gauge" for the effectiveness of New Faith.[2] The economic separation between us has been part of the problem.

### Not Men-Haters

Our connection with brothers is the fourth stage of examination. New Faith wants us to love them without hurting ourselves. We are not haters of men, but we understand that suffering occurs when we love them improperly. Too often we engage in what I term "unnecessary suffering"—foolish behavior patterns in relationships with men. In light of this suffering, New Faith emphasizes that we are ready for relationships with men only after the previous three areas are strong and intact. Historically and culturally this order has been jumbled. The love of men in our lives has always been first; then we tended to the needs of our sisters; the Lord was put in third place, to be summoned in the time of trial. And last and least was us.

New Faith values men. They are our co-creations. We understand that they are wondrous on many levels. A good man is strong arms to hold us. He offers a different point of view to challenge us. His laughter is the base octave that blends with ours. He is a companion for the journey, somebody whom we can trust to do what he says and to always have our back. He prays for us and with us.

Some sisters have lost their "natural minds" attempting to love men. They erroneously worship men as though they were God. Like Jade: "When it came to men, Jade forgot about religion. She was rash and reckless. One Sunday morning while sitting in church, she bowed her head and prayed for her savior to come into her life. She was not praying for Jesus; she wanted a man to save her. When Jade looked up, a handsome brother walked into the sanctuary. "Hallelujah, my prayers have been answered!" she exclaimed.[3]

New Faith is unashamed to state that along with the good ones, there are some bad ones. We identify the bad ones, pray for them, and keep on stepping. We do this because we have options and do not have to settle for less in our relationships. To do all of this and more, New Faith is practical. You won't need a theological dictionary or a master's degree in hermeneutics to become a practitioner of this contemporary faith. You just need two hands. With one hand, hold on to what has been good in your faith experience. New Faith empowers you to use the other hand to work on overcoming the woman-demeaning scriptural interpretations.

## Women and the Black Church

Face it: There is sexism in the Scriptures due to the cultural attitudes of the times. Passages that demand we submit, be silent, and refrain from teaching have been presented in ways to keep us toward the rear of the church leadership. That's why they call us the "backbone of the church."[4] We are expected to go to the back and let the men lead out front.

Face it: Misogyny is rampant in the church. Male pastors routinely tell their female members that if women lead it is a signal that men are weak. In some congregations, "the church organizations prefer slow deterioration under poor male leadership over any female leadership."[5] As a result, proficient, skilled, and competent women remain underused in our pews. Face it: The women who do serve in lay leadership of the church catch hell from other women. It brings out the resentment from deep in the guts of some women to see another woman standing up and stepping out of stereotypical roles. Comments such as "she thinks she's cute" shower women who dare to break the ranks with small dreamers. There is a price to pay for women taking leadership roles.

And women who serve in ministerial capacities can rest assured that other women will be their most ardent foes. Dr. Vashti M. McKenzie in her book *Not without a Struggle* outlines some of the reasons that women block female pastors. She writes, "One of the perennial arguments against female pastors is that it is not the men of the church who object but the women who do not want a woman in the pulpit."[6] According the McKenzie, some of those reasons include that "the pulpit is one of the few remaining positions where women can interact with men who are sensitive to their spiritual needs" and "the pulpit is historically one of the few places African American men can exert strong, positive leadership."[7]

I was the first female pastor appointed to a small congregation, and it was a test case for all. I watched to see how the men handled it; I watched to see how the women handled it. The men mumbled a bit and made peace with my position. The women were checking me out. Mrs. Watson hated my guts. She made it clear the first week I was assigned to the church. "I want a male pastor," she fumed. "What can a woman do for me?" Obviously, there were connections made with previous pastors that I was unable to assist her with. To ensure that I felt uncomfortable and unwanted, she would park her car in my designated parking spot. She would talk loudly to her neighbors during my sermons. She terrorized me and my ministry. Paul talked about his thorn. I had a Mrs. Watson. Paul and I are the stronger because of them.

New Faith underscores the reality that we "are all one in Christ Jesus" (Gal. 3:28). This means that all of us, male or female, can do anything for God and deserve the opportunity to do so with encouragement. Therefore, straighten up, sister: Your bowing-down days are over.

## We Become Students of the Word

As we straighten up, we read and interpret for ourselves. New Faith trains us to interpret what God is saying to us. Listening to a sermon once a week is not enough if you desire change in your life. God speaks to and through any situation. That's the relationship we seek—to hear God speak to us through trial and through joy.

In the New Faith study process we must first understand the context in which the Scriptures were written; then we can distance ourselves from that society. In the same ways that Black men separate themselves from scripture that supports slavery, we identify and reject such scripture that supports the suppression of women. We identify, reject, and rethink what has been interpreted as sexist in the Bible. There is no wrong in calling out the sources of our suffering. If we had a headache and the source of the pain was eating too much pork, we would identify the source, understand that it is harmful, and eliminate it. For too long faith has given us a headache, and we have not understood why. "A major reason that religious faith does not help many women deepen their religious faith and respect for themselves is that most religious traditions have presented patriarchal or male-dominated theologies and ideologies."[8]

As we reexamine our thinking in order to understand what God was saying, we find that God surely did not intend for one race or gender to dominate the other. For example, in the Old Testament world women had the same value as cattle—no voice, no rights. Women were considered to be household items and were listed along with their husbands' other possessions. In Exodus 20:17 we read, "You shall not covet your neighbor's wife or his male servant or his ox or his donkey or anything that belongs to your neighbor." We identify this as sexist and out-of-date thinking. It objectifies women, and therefore we reject the interpretations. God did not create these barriers for women; humans did. We find a better biblical model in a commanding woman like Deborah of Judges 4. She was a woman who happened to be a judge. Deborah was so intrepid and impressive that the mighty warrior Barak was reluctant to go into battle without her. We must rethink the sexist interpretations—their concept of a woman's place is offensive. But our love and respect for God has not changed. God is still God, even though our interpretation of the Bible has changed.

Let's practice again our process of holding on but letting go. Much of the book of Hosea is filled with violent and degrading images of male–female relationships. Hosea repeatedly threatens to harm his wife as punishment for her adultery. He spews, "lest I strip her naked and make her as in the day she was born, and make her like a wilderness, and set her like a parched land and slay her with thirst" (Hos. 2:3). We identify this statement as sexist. His behavior is not wise, sage, or acceptable. She did not drive him to do it; he is wrong. We must reject the violence here because we know that God is a God of peace, and God's laws do not promote abuse of wives.

This lesson is difficult to hear if you love the one who beats you up every weekend. Stephanie's husband sent her back to work every Monday morning covered with bruises. A black eye, a scraped forehead, an elbow that was swollen. Finally Karen, one of my church members who worked with Stephanie, could take it no more. Karen phoned me from work and said in exasperation, "Rev, please help my coworker. Her husband beats her all the time, and she won't leave him!" I said, "I can only help her if she wants to help herself." Eventually I did talk with Stephanie by phone. She explained that her husband was a nice man most of the time, but when he did drugs he "got mean." "Stephanie," I said, "do you understand that your body is a temple of the Lord and that there is no excuse for the temple being beaten?" She began to sob and moan. "He's my husband. He has the right."

In the face of seemingly God-ordained violence, New Faith teaches us to rethink situations and develop intolerance for relationship abuse. New Faith makes it clear that violence against women is never justified. Abuse is ungodly. Let's practice again with a New Testament passage that has been misinterpreted by sexists. In particular, many of the writings of Paul are routinely used. He wrote, "Let women learn in silence with all submissiveness. I permit no woman to teach or to have authority over men; she is to keep silent" (1 Tim. 2:11-12). We must reject the sexist interpretation of this text because of Jesus. It is recorded that he interacted with women—such as Mary and Martha, the woman at the well, and the woman with the alabaster jar—and lifted them up as leaders and spokes-women of the church. Our primary relationship is with God, and this raises us above sexism and any restrictions others present.

Jesus was the gender equalizer. He never stated that women should submit to men or that they should defer leadership positions to men. Jesus came to earth for us all, and when one gender tries to selfishly claim Jesus' author-ity for themselves alone, they sin mightily. Dr. Jacquelyn Grant establishes a strong bond between Jesus and sisters that balances the male-only theology when she writes:

> Jesus Christ thus represents a three-fold significance: first he identifies with the "little people," Black women where they are; secondly, he affirms the basic humanity of these, "the least"; and thirdly, he inspires active hope in the struggle for resurrected, liberated existence.[9]

We are not changing the Bible. We are changing the interpretation of the Bible. You will look at the Bible dif-ferently, however. Our quest for restoration will not let us look at the Bible naively, because it "has been the most consistent and effective book that those in power have used to restrict us and censure the behavior of African American women."[10] Women deserve an experience of interpreting for ourselves. Yes, we can bake our pound cakes, belt out solos, and interpret Scriptures. God talks to us. Let's tell the world what was said. Here's my strat-egy for keeping the faith in the face of scripture and tradi-tion that lessen me: I knew I was somebody in the name of Jesus. I did not feel less endowed with grace or less empowered than any man. I could not stoop to second-class citizenship. I could not go to the back of the bus and accept spiritual segregation. Neither can you. Yes, it is a mental aerobic workout. We hold on and we rethink; we use the brains that God gave us to understand. New Faith requires your mental participation—no more pabulum and no more milk.

## Womanist Theology

A support system for rethinking is womanist theology. Womanist theology is fuel for New Faith. Theology is thoughts about who, what, why, and how God is. Womanist theology gives life to the vision of empowered sisters. New Faith womanist theology is sister-talk about God. It is a relatively new way of expressing ideas about God by Black females who are tired of the church's games.

Alice Walker birthed the word *womanist*. She created it from the "black folk expression mothers used on sassy children."[11] *Womanist* means "outrageous, audacious, courageous, willful women who wanted to know more and in greater depth than is considered good for one."[12] A womanist is one who is responsible and in charge of her everything; her faith, her health, her relationships. She understands that to be pro-herself does not mean that she is anti-anything else. She continually resists attempts to reduce her because of her gender.

I am a womanist because I boldly look through my own eyes and see Jesus for myself. I value the experience I have with him as a Black woman. I was a womanist before I understood there was such a word that described my identity. I am not bound by the "isms." My faith feels exhilarated and empowered. I feel God on my own. It is audacious for sisters to possess an independent relationship with Jesus. He speaks to us and we speak back. Womanist thought helps us eliminate the middleman! It was an epiphany to realize that God was molding and shaping me into a freed woman indeed.

You will discover, as I did, that there is more to God. And if we are to experience it, we must stop waiting on someone to spoon-feed us. Let's seize it. Womanists seize what God has for them and use it for the upbuilding of themselves and others.

Seizing what God has for us can sometimes be a life-saving effort. This is my prayer for Jill. I want her to be in charge of her life. She's given most of it away to her husband, Mark, who abuses her with infidelity, deceit, and trickery. Jill became pregnant, and the two of them were pressured into getting married a lot sooner than they would have liked to. The pressure came from the seminary where they both were enrolled. Just weeks prior to the wedding day, Jill found Mark in bed with another woman. He swore that he'd never cheat again. Jill believed him, and the wedding took place as scheduled. During their first year of marriage, however, she caught him in the act with women several times. It would be predictable to blame Mark. But New Faith encourages Jill to claim her relationship with Jesus as primary and relinquish her unfaithful man. We must take responsibility for our own actions.

Womanist theology emerged in the 1970s as sister theologians grew weary of hearing others speak for them about God. They chafed under language designed for others. Imagine this: A question is presented to you, but before you can answer it, an Anglo woman or man or an African American man speaks on your behalf. Your opinions are not heard and do not matter. Imagine that this keeps happening over and over again, so much so that the thoughts of African American women are considered immaterial. This is what happened to our sisters in theological circles. Others spoke for them. We don't need anyone else other than ourselves to speak for us. Allow me to introduce you to just a few of these sister theologians and some of their books. Please see page 160 for a suggested-reading list.

Womanist theology helps us make sense of our situation. We've survived on hand-me-downs, leftovers, and scraps from other people for too long. Feminism has tried to address our situation. Feminist theology is the White woman's perspective of God and how God works in their lives. I have no qualms with it—it works for them. White women need their own interpretation, as do we. Liberation theology has tried to address our situation. It is the perspective of Third World and African American men; I have no qualms with it, either. They need their own interpretation. African American men and White women are well taken care of theologically. Who is taking care of our theological needs? We need our own thing. It is our responsibility to do theology our way.

## The Power of Words

Let's be in charge of our theology. Let's be in charge of our words. Words have an impact on our world. Did you know that words direct our psyche and our soul? They quietly and forcefully sculpt our ways of interpreting our surroundings. Some words like *queen* build us up. Other words like *bitch* break us down.

There is an unforgettable scene in the movie *The Color Purple* when that wicked character Mister (portrayed by Danny Glover) wanted to throw more salt onto the gaping emotional wounds of his downtrodden wife, Celie (portrayed by Whoopi Goldberg). Mister pummels Celie with a litany of insults. His words escalating as they came, he screamed, "You're Black, po', you skinny, and you a woman. Goddam . . . you nothing at all."[13]

The language of the church pummels us in a similar fashion. It is steeped in "masculine language." All that is male is exalted. Masculine language shapes our understanding to the degree that if God is male, then male is God. Think about the hymns we sing, such as "Rise Up, O Men Of God," "Faith of Our Fathers," and "This is My Father's World." Ask yourself why have you only heard male pronouns for God when the Bible tells us that God is both male and female? ". . . In the image of God he created them; male and female he created them" (Gen. 1:27; NRSV). Deep down inside, some of us believe that being a woman is the worst thing we can be. New Faith rescues us with words that heal and restore. Inclusive words for God are the foundation of New Faith. Inclusive words for God present God as the Bible does, as both male and female. They broaden our images and understandings of God. They offer us vocabulary options we need to gain access to more truth.

### God Is More than Father

As quiet as it is kept, God is more than a father; God is also a midwife. In Isaiah 66:9 we are told, "'Shall I bring to the birth and not cause to bring forth?' says the LORD." In Psalm 22:9-11 we hear, "Yet thou art he who took me from the womb; thou didst keep me safe upon my mother's breasts." God also has the image of a protective mother. Isaiah 66:13 says "As a mother comforts her child, so I will comfort you; you shall be comforted in Jerusalem" (NRSV).

My favorite image is of God as a mother hen, fiercely protective and efficient. Two Scripture passages present this image. In Psalm 36:7 we read, "How precious is your steadfast love, O God! All people may take refuge in the shadow of your wings" (NRSV). And Matthew 23:37 tells us, "O Jerusalem, Jerusalem, killing the prophets and stoning those who are sent to you! How often would I have gathered your children together as a hen gathers her brood under her wings, and you would not!"

Sisters, I believe that the use of inclusive language gives our relationships with God, ourselves, and others a sane foundation, replacing the madness that existed before. With inclusive language we can love and be loved without hurting ourselves. Many of us have wounds from abusive authority figures (fathers, brothers, pastors, and teachers). These wounds make it painful and confusing to love a male God. What we actually possess is a twisted, perverted love that keeps us hurting all the time. New Faith sets us free with inclusive language.

## Just Knowing Jesus

Black women have loved Jesus for a long time. For us Jesus has always been the only real necessity. Many a sister declared, "Just give me Jesus!" Just knowing Jesus made sisters bold back in the day. It was enough just to know who he was. He was the Alpha and the Omega for brave abolitionist Sojourner Truth. "When asked by a preacher if the source of her preaching was the Bible, she responded, 'No honey, can't preach from de Bible—can't read a letter.' Then she explained: 'When I preaches, I has jest one text to preach from an I always preaches from this one. My text is When I found Jesus.'"[14]

Yes, sisters have always loved them some Jesus and in an interesting myriad of ways. He is the man we love to sing about: "Can't Nobody Do Me Like Jesus" and "O How I Love Jesus." We have powerful verbiage about Jesus, too. He's the "rock in the weary land," the "shelter in the time of storm," "Mary's baby," "the prince of peace," "the bright morning star." We know him as the superstar of Easter morning and the central figure of Christmas day. We love him because we share the same address, between a rock and a hard place. We have a historical link to him with the hard times we experience. He knew what it meant to be an outcast; so do we. He knew the heartache of rejection; so do we. He was talked about and humiliated, just as we have been.

We need even more reasons to love him in this millennium. We've got to love him for his boldness. Jesus is my license to be bold. I rejected that old notion of being meek and mild as a follower of Jesus. I embrace the freedom fighter, not the status quo enforcer. His resurrection means that "there is more to life than the cross. Our hard times are not our end."[15]

Jesus is the epicenter of my belief system. I can do anything because he lives. I draw power from my association with him. Jesus died on Calvary for me. That means I am special, not common. I am a conqueror and not a victim. This I take personally. I take Jesus literally and not figuratively. Therefore my spirit is insulted by limited interpretations of Christianity for women. It hurts me to meet young women who have absorbed the sexist culture and are growing up crooked and bent over. That's exactly what happened once at a women's college, I was told. The college minister shared with me that one day during chapel services she used the female pronoun for God. After the service a throng of students flooded her office. "Why did you call God a woman?" "Are you crazy?" "Don't you know better?" they asked. In their young minds God was who they said he was. New Faith dares us to think, see, and tell who God actually is.

Years ago there was a popular recording that said, "What you see is what you get." This is true about our belief system. What we see, hear, and absorb within the faith experience on Sundays directly affects our faith system. Sisters, we have a choice. We can accept the minority report that confirms we are inferior. Or we can believe that Jesus died on the cross for our full womanhood. You are good and grown: Choose for yourself. Does your church provide an atmosphere for your belief system to grow? Or are you boxed in? What do you see around you that supports a convincing presentation of women? If you do not see women in leadership, how does that affect your faith?

New Faith boldly asks us, "Do we really know Jesus? Do we know him in his revolutionary responses to women?" He is a role model for the treatment of women. He wouldn't put a woman out of his pulpit. He wouldn't mind if the visiting preacher wore a skirt or pants, he'd just want to hear the Word! New Faith tells us that to love him means we've got to know the true Jesus for ourselves. He is on our side. We can be brave because he has our backs.

Jesus broke down the walls of sexism with his equal treatment of women. He is our hero because he was intolerant of prejudice, sexism, and any other type of wrong. When Jesus met the woman with the issue of blood, he did not recoil in horror from her touch. Women who were menstruating were labeled "dirty." They were restricted from public outings and were not to be touched. But when she touched Jesus, he commended her faith. That tells us that Jesus was about breaking up the good ol' boy club.

Sisters, you are all right just as you are. Your womanness, menstrual cycle, and other female concerns are not problematic. They are a part of the package that God made and declared good. When Jesus came to the home of Martha and Mary (Luke 10:38), he showed them and the men present that women's work has no limits. He pointed out other options for women, rather than confining them to housework.

Sisters, Jesus is saying that sometimes cooking and cleaning can wait. Studying his word, preaching, teaching, and leading are our jobs, too. When Jesus chose the female disciples (Luke 8), he taught society that women have worth as ministers, pastors, and spiritual leaders. Those sisters traveled with him and the male disciples. They had a place of power and prominence in the work of Jesus. This models the correct ways for male and female clergy to understand themselves. There is room for us all.

What does Jesus mean to us today in New Faith? It means that we can take off those ridiculous blinders installed by sexism and understand that Jesus died for the sins of the world—not just the men, not just the women, but for all of us! Christ offers us "universal salvation."[16] This means that Christ died on the cross for men and women. We have equal access and equal blessings.

New Faith gives us use of the broad-based nature of Christ. It keeps us off the narrow ledge of rigid literalism.

It is key that Jesus is identified with more than one type of injustice. It is easy to spot racism, pursue it, and ignore the other sins. This is what has happened with the civil rights movement. The courageous leaders were correct to challenge racism in all its vile forms. Yet in their obsession to correct the White man's error, they conveniently overlooked their own smoldering sexism. How can one fight racism all day, come home, and perpetuate sexism all night? Knowing Jesus the right way urges us to demand a larger slice of the pie of power and influence in our churches. This understanding marches us out of the kitchen and up to the front chair in the pastor's boardroom for decision making. Jesus is on our side.

## We Ain't Going Anywhere

Let me be perfectly clear. Even though the Bible is fraught with sexist thought and interpretation, even though the church perpetuates it, we are not leaving. We are not going anywhere. The church is ours, and here we shall stay. But who can rest peacefully in a dirty house? We have got some work to do! Equipped with New Faith we must become "house revolutionaries."[17] Our goal is to make radical changes from the inside out. As "house revolutionaries," we are like Jesus in the temple. We do not wish to destroy the house of authority; quite the contrary, we "wish to build it up again as a new house," where we are somebody, too.[18] We have much to do. Get up. Keep strutting on.

## Reflection Questions

1. Have you seen misogyny in your church?
2. How can you reject sexist interpretations of Scripture?
3. What is a womanist to you?
4. Who is Jesus to you?

# 3. My Soul Looks Back

"[God] restores my soul." (Psalm 23:3)

**When my soul** looks back into the past, it sees itself strong, glorious, and loved. My soul is more like a Nubian royal surveying her rolling Serengeti in the coolness of an African dusk rather than like the ever-toiling mammy who in the blazing noonday heat is nursing her brood, plus massa's, as she churns butter and bakes biscuits. My soul clings to its African roots for strength. There my ancient sisters were draped in regal Kente fabrics and donned in gold from their own mines. In many African societies women were wealthy, powerful merchants and landowners. Our royalness goes back, way back. We have antiquity awesome.

You see, my soul looks back to sisters such as Nefertiti, the wife of Amenhotep IV. She played an active role in shaping Black Egypt between 1365 and 1352 BCE. There was Hatshepsut, who, after the death of her husband, Thutmose II, took full control of the throne. She stabilized Egypt during a season of peace for more than twenty years. Hatshepsut established a new style of female leadership by wearing male clothes. This awesome woman of ancient times was addressed by her subjects not as "Her Majesty the Queen" but as "Her Majesty the King." Centuries later Nzinga became queen of what is now Angola in 1623. She found herself constantly at war with the Portuguese, and according to Dutch observers, at the age of sixty she was still leading her warriors into battle.[1]

In the Scriptures we have her royalness "the Candace," who is the queen of Ethiopia. We learn about her in Acts 8:25-40 when we meet "the Ethiopian eunuch, court official of Candace, queen of the Ethiopians." He is on the desert road outside of Jerusalem doing his queen's bidding. *Candace* is actually the term given to a lineage of African female leadership of Ethiopia from 1000 BCE to 1000 CE. The Candace produced exceptional palaces, tombs, statues, and other edifices. These images give us the feeling of assurance, grace, and achievement. Regrettably, many of my sisters don't feel assured and fortified. They are living like slave women because a sinister authority known as the church indentures them. Their souls have been fettered and pinned down. I know why. They have not looked back far enough.

## Healing History

It is a luxury of the twenty-first century to look retrospectively. There is soul healing there. When we look back with New Faith, the past is no longer *their* history but *our* history—"herstory." Herstory has a way of liberating. It is the truth, and the truth will set us free. We can be free from what people said we were and what we were not. The past has not always been kind. Yes, there has been heartache, headaches, and hassles in yesterday. Yet we must look.

Most important, in New Faith we review the facts and interpret for ourselves. How did we get this way? Has faithful churchgoing helped us or hurt us? Looking back gives us the guts to ask questions our foremothers never dared, such as: Are the stained-glass walls in many sanctuaries acting as sacred barriers keeping women in their prescribed place in the pews? Does the sexist rhetoric flowing from pulpits stifle female congregants and create a climate of fear for any woman who steps out of line and acknowledges her call into ministry? Why have generations of women been  told who they were and who they were not? Why have we all agreed in the name of Jesus to be girls in God's house? It's as if our souls are still on the plantations. The church has created elements that keep the souls of women enslaved on plantations. Many of us have no idea that we are better than that.

Here's the story of one sister whose soul was still on the plantation. Martha's voice is a trumpet of authority and command. When she speaks, people listen. As executive director of a prominent women's advocacy organization, she is in total control. The budget hasn't seen red due to her financial prowess. The personnel department is no longer rocked by scandal; she knows how to manage people. The organization's future is bright because with her premium training she plans for anticipated shifts in the years to come.

Powerful women are often perceived as threats. Behind Martha's back her subordinates call her names like "bossy," "Miss Attitude," and "Queen Bitch." They respect her reign of control, however. Once, a businessman visiting the office made the mistake of addressing Martha as a drone rather than the queen that she is. This disrespect to the queendom was neutered in a flash because sister hit the roof. She claimed who she was and corrected the offending party in the middle of a meeting. "No one talks to me like that," she snapped. "I've earned my title, my position, and my salary. I will not be undermined. Don't you know who I am? Lord knows all the years I spent in school, the jobs I worked just to get where I am." Rather than upbraid him further, Martha barked, "Meeting adjourned." Abruptly she pivoted and stormed into her office. Behind the closed door, she scooped up her Bible to calm herself. "I can do all things through Christ, who strengthens me." She chanted and breathed a sigh of relief. "I can do this. I can do this. Sexism moves out of my way. I am God's woman," she whispered quietly to herself.

Martha is an incredibly capable woman six days a week. With the sunrise of Sunday dawns a different persona. She sheds the dominance and dons the submission. She sheds her managerial style for the need to be managed. Gospel music marches through the air of her home as she prepares for worship service: "Lord, help me to hold out." Martha believes that the music lifts her, but it also anaesthetizes her as she prepares to enter another world where her other self is out of order and biblically wrong. It matters not that Martha is degreed, a community leader, and a CEO. At church, she is a girl who takes orders, and thus she will fall in line with others. On the grounds of Greater Memorial, pleasing the pastor is uppermost. She bows, scrapes, and genuflects like the others. She's been trained for it: "Momma taught me to serve the pastor." Sitting in the pews, Martha eagerly hears and internalizes sermons that are a direct contradiction of who she is. A woman's role is to help, not lead. "Amen, preacher," she yells. If God wanted women to run anything, He'd have made them first! "Hallelujah, Jesus," Martha bellows. After service she heads for the kitchen to offer additional service. The finance room and trustee rooms are off limits. She understands that women serve—not lead. Women listen—not teach.

Martha is devoted to her faith, and as a result she is a victim of her faith. She is a melting woman, a sister who allows her devotion to misogynist teachings to strip away her personhood. In effect she dissolves slowly, bit by bit under the caustic drip of the faith that she's always known and loved. She is experiencing the effects of unnecessary suffering. This affliction of Christian women is handed down from one generation to the next like a prized set of china. Martha is not alone. She is legion. How did it all begin?

## Slavery and Christianity

In the 1700s Portuguese shippers added slaves to their trading commerce. Indentured servitude for us was the beginning of physical destruction that I would argue ultimately damaged our souls more than our bodies. In slavery, women of African descent were locked within the intersection of religion, gender, racial, and class oppression of tremendous magnitude. Christianity was the conduit of oppression for all slaves. It affected women in particularly vicious ways. Upon arrival in America, slaves were baptized and ushered into Christianity by their owners for purposes of control. The slave masters employed an array of tools for submission, including whips and shackles. Yet their use of Christianity was more potent than the physical measures of control. The Bible led slaves to accept their fate. And "some masters became convinced that some of the best slaves—that is, those amiable to control by their white masters—were those who read the Bible."[2] The masters taught the slaves a racist religion that encouraged them to accept their lowered status and miserable conditions and to be cooperative with superiors.

In boldness that only accompanies maturity, the slave church eventually shunned the racist, controlling interpretations of Christianity that were given by their masters. The slave church was the only element of their existence within their control. The slaves soon grew to love the God of Moses who liberated the Hebrew slaves. They loved the Jesus who was rebuked and scorned through no fault of his own. These slave churches complete with slave preachers developed into our first and still our most viable institution. The church became a springboard of resistance, as evidenced by the musical genre known as "spirituals." "Wade in the Water" was a message of escape from the plantation toward freedom in the north. "Swing Low, Sweet Chariot" was a message from God that someday relief from suffering would come.

While the slave church clearly identified racist mistreatment and promised God's vengeance on the oppressors, its vision seemed blurred regarding the inequity of women's roles. While women were expected to carry the same amount of labor in the fields, women's roles in religion were minimal and subjugated. I suggest that this injustice caused Christianity to be a bittersweet experience for our sisters. From today's perspective, looking back on the slaves' brush arbor worship services or prayer meetings by the riverside, I wonder: Were my sisters disturbed about their situation? They shouted "Amen" to the Word of God but had to repress the reality of their mistreatment. They were expected to embrace the message of Christ but ignore the meanness directed at them. Patriarchy and enslavement placed Black women in a vacuum of personhood.

Into this coarse mix was added sexual abuse of slave women. One slave woman shared this account: "My sister was given away when she was a girl. She told me and ma that they'd make her go out and lay on a table and two or three white men would have sex with her before they'd let her get up. She was just a small girl. She died when she was still in her young days, still a girl."[3] Slave women found themselves defenseless elements in an iniquitous equation that included "the church, the operating laws of capitalism, and the psychological needs of White males."[4] The slave men were absent from this equation. The souls of the sisters must have ached as they witnessed the castration of their men. It is natural to assume that the slave women wanted their men to function like the Scripture heroes who defended their families and protected their women in times of distress.

Perhaps the slave women envisioned warrior men similar to those in 1 Sam. 18:6, who went off to fight enemies and were celebrated by their women upon a victorious homecoming. But the enslaved men could not protect their women because they could not protect themselves. Slave women fended for themselves; circumstances dictated that they be strong, aggressive, and dominating. As a result, slave women were central figures in slave families. Going against the grain of patriarchy, slave women often held the role of rescuers and defenders of their men.

The context of slavery victimized both men and women. There is no need for either gender to compete for the prize of the greatest accumulation of pain and most degrading effects. Slavery's horrors emotionally separated men from women. The women fiercely loved their men and sought a means of making sense of their predicament. Their answer came from the slave church. It offered a framework for their understanding. The slave women's desire to help their men birthed an arrangement in which the women lowered themselves in order to lift up their men. This self-sacrifice was understood to be biblically correct and necessary for harmonious relationships.

The slave women also turned aside the concerns over sexism. It was too great a luxury to focus on self when the entire race lived under tremendous subjugation. In return for the sacrifice of selves, the women hoped their men would be able and willing to rescue, love, and protect them. Unnecessary suffering was born in this complicated merger of misery, love, and faith. Christianity spoke to the slave woman's situation. Christianity was all that they had. The more the women embraced the faith, the greater the spiritual fervor they experienced. In return they were increasingly willing to sacrifice themselves. One theologian describes it thus:

God and religion fulfilled some very basic needs that could not be fulfilled by the slave community or the black man. Thus slave narratives often portray black mothers exhibiting a vigorous spiritualist self-confidence even though their sexuality has been completely brutalized and exploited.[5]

## The Past Colors Our Present

The truth that women love men who degrade them, abandon them, cuss at them, strike them, and cheat on them is a result of what our foremothers did or failed to do. We are not angry. We are aware that they did the best they could. We hold no grudges against their deeds. Truth is truth. New Faith does not squander time on what cannot be changed. It's been stated that "religion is the single most important shaper and enforcer of the image and role of women in culture and society."[6] The images and roles of women that come to us from the context of plantation Christianity are troubling. The history of enslaved Black Christian women, rather than our glorious pre-slavery past, colors our present circumstances. An indelible dye was cast upon us during slavery. Our souls were primed to flow in an unnatural spiritual direction. We have embraced and exalted suffering. Suffering is a destructive yet prominent feature of contemporary Black Christian womanhood.

It must be noted that Black women are not alone in this area. White women also have found value in excessive self-denial. The difference is that in the crucible of slavery the suffering of slave women was intimately acquainted with greater depths of agony.

. . . The idealization and romanticization of Black women's suffering is as insidious a habit in the African American community as it has been historically in the dominant society. Elevating women's suffering to a form of martyrdom for the cause (of others) virtually guarantees that it will remain unexamined. Herein lies a peculiar dilemma for our community. On the one hand, women's suffering is apotheosized [given divine status]. By doing so, we subscribe to the suffering-servant motif in Christology. On the other hand, if the proximate cause of the suffering is the men within the community, the response of the community is active or passive denial.[7]

Contemporary Black Christian women, though freed from physical fetters, remain religiously affixed to gender limitations and gender-specific religious abuse. The absence of women in church leadership often goes without question. It is a welcome sign that Black men are strong and in control. In a contorted sense, Black women seem to find relief in the context of men being solely in charge. This perplexing voluntary submission has its roots in the ways that Black women view the Bible. Many Black women accept everything in Scripture as is. These women feel that they cannot interpret God's word for themselves (as Sojourner Truth did). Instead of being freed by Scripture, they are bound by it. African American women understand Paul's command to be submissive to their husbands as a scriptural mandate to stay in physically and emotionally abusive relationships in their own homes as well as outside them. They understand their plight as God's will.

What does this mean for you and me today? Take a look around and see for yourself that the contemporary Black church remains largely sexist. Yes, there are bright places. We have had two African American female bishops in mainstream Protestant denominations. Bishop Barbara Harris was elected a bishop of the Episcopal Church in 1984. Bishop Leontyne T. C. Kelly was elected a bishop of the United Methodist Church in 1984. It is good news that there are thousands of clergywomen

across America. Some hold the position of senior pastor
or associate pastor. There are also at least two dozen
clergywomen who are pastors of congregations that
exceed 1,000 members. These sisters have nationally
known ministries and books and they receive wide
acclaim as God's true messengers.

A major indication of African American clergywoman's
status can be found in *Ebony* magazine. This revered peri-
odical has been an icon of the Black community since
1945. In 1998 Ebony began listing America's "Top Ten
Clergywomen," along with its "Top Ten Clergymen." This
is progress. It is also exciting to learn that there are seminaries across the nation swelling with women students. In
response, seminaries and schools of theology offer cours-
es that affirm women, such as classes on womanist and
feminist theology.

Despite significant gains, sexism looms large. The two
elected bishops have retired and have not been replaced.
It should also be noted that these two sisters were lifted
up within predominantly Anglo denominations. Why
haven't the African American denominations that ordain
women such as the African Methodist Episcopal (AME),
AME Zion, or Christian Methodist Episcopal (CME)
elected women for the episcopacy? Moreover, even
though women are serving in church leadership, more
often than not they are associate pastors. Women in the
position of senior pastor, particularly in large churches,
are few and far between. The salaries of female clergy
continue to trail behind male clergy. And when those
thousands of female seminarians graduate, what will they
find? Will there be pulpit committees that seek them out,
or will they be limited to associate positions when they
prefer to be senior pastor?

There is a by-product of sexism that afflicts women who
are in the early stages of realizing their call to ministry.
They may be enrolled in seminary or still sitting in the

pews. Such women rarely see themselves as called to be pastors. Often I am asked to mentor sister seminarians. Without fail the women will adamantly declare they are not seeking the job of pastor. "I just want to counsel"; "I just want to teach"; "I just want to be an administrator." One sister, who is now a university chaplain, described her hesitation: "I could not see myself in that role. My picture did not go with the word *pastor*. Something was wrong with that picture," she recalled. Sexism is also seen in the situation of women whose ministerial aspirations are constantly wrestled to the ground of the church. Some male pastors pummel their women back into the pews by wielding one out-of-context passage (Paul's infamous "I do not permit women to teach men" [2 Tim. 2:12]).

Carol called me and invited me to lunch. I did not know her, but her voice was flooded with need. I did not know it, but she needed my help to plot her escape from the hostile climate of a plantationlike existence. At first glance she appeared to be a mature, intelligent woman. Yet it seemed that something impenetrable was holding her back from entering ministry. "I know that God has called me to preach, but I am afraid to tell my pastor," said the fifty-year-old woman. "I'm his secretary, and I know how he feels about women who try to be pastors. It's not right according to him. But I know what the Lord told me. How do I follow God and follow my pastor?" I encouraged Carol to follow the Lord and not her pastor. New Faith offers women like Carol something to stand on other than the same old tired theology of limitation. "I endorse your love and respect for him, but where," I asked, "do you draw the line between supporting the pastor and laying down your life, hopes, and dreams for him? Stop waiting on his approval. God has already approved you," I said.

## Too Much Focus on Fashion

In other instances the church's sexism is seen in the fashion ghettos that confine women. Instead of making decisions about church property and bank accounts, women are "encouraged to be concerned with their clothes."[8] In some Black churches the clothing ensembles of the in-house fashion maven is of more importance than the pastor's sermon. "Girl, did you see what she had on?" is more frequently asked than "did you receive a blessing from the service?" When what a woman wears is the only means of her gaining status in the church community, then truly there is an "over-valuation of appearance in black life."[9]

Here's what I mean. Christy's suit alone cost $2,000. Matching to a T are a purse, shoes, and a hat. The most outrageously priced item that completes the ensemble is the $150 sequined handkerchief. This outfit has set her back three paychecks, but it matters not. Primping in the mirror on Sunday morning, Christy grins to herself: "I can't let the others out-dress me. Now, the service starts at eleven. If I get there by noon, that's perfect timing to make the offering. I'll stroll slowly up the center aisle, nod to the pastor, wink at the first lady, and roll my eyes at the two hens sitting in the front row. They think they can dress, but they have not seen me," she schemes. "Oh," she pauses, "but if I get there by eleven-thirty, I can make the testimony time. They can see me strut twice. I'd better hurry."

Christy's soul has been held hostage. Her power is in her closet. She serves on no committees, makes no decisions, and leads no one. The highest that she can achieve is marked by the cloth on her back. New Faith would give her so much confidence in herself that she could come to church in blue jeans with her head held high because she found the real reason to strut. This author is not anti-style, elegance, and glamour. The panache of the African American church woman is legendary. It should continue if we understand that we must do more than just look good, lest we elegantly slip into the role of ornamentation. Sitting there looking too pretty to do anything but sit there and look pretty perpetuates the patriarchy. Our dazzling outfits should be matched by our dazzling leadership contributions.

## The Backbone of the Church

The pervasive sexism that I speak of means those Black women have been and still are the backbone of the church. They have remained loyal workers and supporters. Long ago I thought this a compliment because the backbone or spine has a major role in the body. But the scenarios shared above tell us that the term *backbone* actually references "location rather than function. What they really meant is that women are in the background and should be kept there. They are merely support workers."[10]

Theologian sisters have written about the reality and impact of sexism. Delores Williams asserts that Christianity has failed the Black Christian woman because it has "confounded her understanding of black suffering and has caused her to accept untenable explanations for it."[11] I disagree: Christianity has not failed us; Jesus Christ cannot fail us. The historical sexist interpretations have failed us. New Faith enables us to see this truth based on our analysis of our past. Christ serves as the anchor for our souls. Restoration from the Lord holds us firmly when all around us is shaking. This anchor keeps us where we were meant to be when the winds of opposition want to move us. Our souls have travailed through history. It is only because of Christ that we are still here. Despite all of our suffering, our souls know that we are queens, not mammies.

Queens, see who you really are. You are royal every-where you go. The same power you wield at home, at school, and on the job travels with you into the church house. Do not park your power at the door any longer. Lean back in your chaise lounge of confidence. Survey the rolling Serengeti of your life, and smile. New Faith won't let you be who they tell you you are. Your faith won't hold you back, trip you up, or cut you short again. New Faith is taking you somewhere. It's a place you've never been before, but our souls have known we belonged there all the while.

## Reflection Questions

1. Has suffering been passed down to you in your family?
2. What did slavery and the slave church do to Black women?
3. What does *backbone* mean to you?
4. Does an obsession with clothes distract us from the Lord?

# **4** Revising Ourselves

"So if anyone is in Christ, there is a new creation: every-thing old has passed away; see, everything has become new!" (2 Cor. 5:17 NRSV)

**Before we can change** this wayward world, we must change ourselves. New Faith teaches us that a revised self is a blessed self. To embrace a stagnant lifestyle is insanity. Nothing should stay the same. The Scriptures say that newness comes from Christ. That is surely talking about us. We are women who have the guts to premeditate a holy metamorphosis. Revision is edu-cated, calculated transformation from the inside out. A revision is more than a makeover. It is more powerful than changing your wardrobe because of climatic alter-ations. It is more profound than rearranging the furniture in your house. It is an internal, psychological, sociologi-cal, christological turn. Revision means endurance. It lasts longer than a color rinse or the latest "do." It is not a fad, a trend, or a popular way of doing things. In fact your revision may make you vastly unpopular. But you are not revising for others. (And you've already agreed to walk counter-culture.) Come on—you are revising for God.

## Old Ways, New Ways

Unless the Lord is a part of your new edition, it is all for naught. Can you dare to become who God wants you to be? If not, you will stay locked in the past like some church women who invited me to their church for a Saturday morning seminar. They were inmates at the Christian prison of the past, and they seemed to love it. My invitation to their church was to present a workshop on women's issues. It promised to be an uncomplicated event. Yet when the sole of my navy-blue suede pump touched the asphalt of their church parking lot, I was certain that their revision was way overdue. An ancient jolt jetted up from my heel to my head because my surroundings were obsolete. The church women and their ways were ancient. Their pastor and his ways reeked of the past. My clues? The women all wore dresses, as though pants would be a one-way ticket to hell. The pastor bristled when I introduced myself as Reverend Patterson, not "evangelist" Patterson.

A quick tour of the church gave me the private opportunity to ask one of the women about the name of the church. It had two last names. That puzzled me. It was something like the "Smith-Jones" Church. The sister tour guide proudly explained that two dedicated women founded the church. The worship services were held in the homes of these women. "They baked pies and fried chicken to build the church," she detailed with pride.

"Wow," I exclaimed. "The church is named after them."

"No," she paused and looked away sheepishly. "The church is named after the founders' husbands. Women around here have to step back and let men lead," she said matter-of-factly.

Yes, it was the modern day, but it was old ways and time for a revision. I wanted to snatch up the women of this church by the lapels of their white dresses and scream, "Run! Danger!" But the congealed stare of the pastor and the timid expressions of the women confirmed there would be nothing new going on in that place—at least not that day.

Historically, change was not in our vocabulary. Our foremothers did not have the authority to grow in new directions. The same was all they had permission to have. In this millennium, we can no longer afford sameness. Our tolerance of the status quo is our greatest liability. We must employ corrective love if we are to change.

## Corrective Love

Corrective love begins at home, before it can be employed with others. Corrective love is a combination of the love of God and the love of self. You change yourself with the love of God. Yes, God is in control. Our role is being open to God's movement. Jesus offered a corrective love, too. When he met the woman at the well, he knew that she could not stay the same. She became a new woman as she recognized her worth, the worthlessness of her behavior, and the power of Jesus in her. When Jesus encountered the woman caught in adultery, he knew that she could not remain the same. She became a new woman as she recognized her worth despite her sins. She was changed. We too cannot remain the same.

Jesus is looking at us, knowing that we cannot remain the same. He may wonder, Can we recognize our worth? It is difficult to feel expensive when devaluation is the air that we breathe. Sociologists report that African American women are "the most disadvantaged group in the United States."[1] We are the "poorest paid workers, have shorter life expectancies than females of other races, have higher infant mortality rates, are more likely to contract stress-related diseases, are more likely to be diagnosed as having chronic rather than acute mental illness, and are more likely to be institutionalized for mental illness."[2] Mental health experts also view our condition seriously, indicating that we have the "lowest level of emotional well-being across the sex and race [categories] with reports of moderate to severe levels of stress."[3] Stress is defined as "a function or degree to which any environmental demand/stimuli taxes or exceeds one's resources to cope with or overcome it."[4] You know this problem as that which works your last nerve. Some of the stressors facing us are: "inadequate resources, relationship conflict/dissatisfaction, racism/ethnicity, loss or disappointment, hysterectomy, pregnancy and marriage. . . ."[5]

This is not what God plans for us. Negative factors are like putrid trash stacking up in our lives. Change means emptying the trash. We have heaps of trash in our lives that prevent our revision. We must gather it up and leave it by the curb for the garbage collector. If we move it away from us, the effects will be diminished.

Allow me to identify the issues in our trash: Sexism affects us. It's the smelly substance that we grew up with, and it won't go away. We have become accustomed to its presence and made space for it in our lives. In small yet insidious ways sexism keeps women of God chasing meaningless issues and keeps them distracted from their destinies. For example, many women are prisoners to makeup. Facial cosmetics are not an evil, but if we understand ourselves to be presentable only when we are covered in cosmetics, this thinking is evil. It keeps us locked in others' perceptions. Men do not preoccupy themselves with color-coordinated cheeks, lips, and eyelids. We perpetually dash to salons for manicures and pedicures to keep our hands and feet presentable to those who in return do not offer us painted anything. Revise. Free yourself and find inner, natural beauty. Revision for some of us will mean coming out from behind the makeup to dress and appear as we like.

Racism affects us, too. Racism is so powerful, it will make you hate yourself secretly. The intense hatred from others can penetrate inside your spirit, launch an internal war, and recruit you as the chief of destruction. Self-hatred is in your life if you admit to committing self-sabotage. Do you do things to keep yourself down? Do you convince yourself that your thoughts are no good, your efforts meaningless? The effects of racism, our constant companion, can be overcome. No, you can't change every racist, but you can change your reaction to them. Revise, and examine the ways in which you hold yourself back. Remove your hands from your neck. Lift your boot off your back. Look at your deepest fears, and stare them down until you accomplish what God has destined for you.

Classism affects us: It keeps us on the bottom of the economic ladder. The oppressive hand of economic inequity seeks to ensure that we don't have a proverbial "pot to put anything in or a window to throw it out of." A broke woman is a powerless woman. Revise, wise up, and learn the skill of money management. Budget the money you have, set small financial goals and meet them, build home equity instead of throwing it away in rent, and someday invest in money market accounts and mutual funds.

The fourth heap of trash in your midst is ageism. This is the one no sister really wants to discuss. Getting older is one of those silent oppressors that won't leave us alone. In our society aging is a curse. Women spend millions annually to keep their teenage figures and faces. Going gray may be the symbol of wisdom and maturity on a man, but it is the kiss of death for a woman. Aging sentences her to the world of hair dyes and girdles. Revise; celebrate each birthday as it is, a gift from God. You know, as I know—God did not have to do it, but since she did, seize each year with gusto and pride. Each year you are given by God deserves to be celebrated, not denied. We should be tired of being somebody's statistic. Change is no longer an option; revision is mandatory. We must undergo revision if we are to survive. The future is intolerant of our sameness.

Don't be duped into staying the same. You can change and still love Jesus. Your love for him and faith in his power are not damaged or threatened by your changing. It's O.K. to be somebody new in Jesus. He does not want us to be the same old folk we were way back when. Who benefits by your clinging to the past? Certainly not you.

You know you need revision if:
- you believe that supporting women's issues makes you anti-male
- you resent women who follow their dreams rather than others' opinions
- you believe that Jesus and God are a couple of white guys
- you refuse to embrace the feminine side of God
- you believe that your pastor is the only theologian you need
- you believe that wives are a helpmeet, a.k.a. doormat
- you believe that women can't preach like men
- you believe that women are the only ones who should take care of children
- you believe that submission is a woman's duty
- you believe that women can't teach men.

Revision begins with the belief that knowledge of the self is primary. Talk about resistance! I raised this issue at a woman's prayer breakfast, and one sister nearly got whiplash by jerking her neck around. "Learn myself?" she bellowed with belligerence. "Find some other topic!" Her reaction is understandable. It is threatening to delve into the deep, dark self. There are no lights down there, no map, no guide—and hence no concern. It's a place where we have not been. Why are we afraid? We don't know what to do with what we learn. We fear what it will do to us. Besides, it's easy to major in everyone's business but our own.

I enjoy offering counseling to couples contemplating marriage. The initial counseling session is always a "getting to know you" time. Occasionally, as I strive to gather information about the couple, it becomes clear that the prospective bride and groom do not know themselves. I ask the couples primary questions about self such as: What are your strengths? What are your weaknesses? What future plans do you have? What event in your past has had the greatest impact on your present?

In one particular couple, both thirty years old, the woman was clueless about who she was. There was a blank expression on her face when she was asked about her personal strengths and weaknesses. She stalled when I pressed her for answers. Although her fiancé glibly rattled off his answers, she was dumbfounded and finally confessed, "I don't know. I've never taken the time to think about me. I know about the kids, school, my fiancé, but nothing about me. I don't know me. It was never important," she said.

Revision will come to each of us. Experience has taught me that there are two ways to revise ourselves; by choice or by force. The first way is the most preferable. Such a sister understands the statement in Ecclesiastes 3:1 that there is a time and place for everything under heaven. She is not bothered with the discomforts of change, and she determines what must be done and does it. She does not want to be left behind.

Annette began to realize that the pattern of her life was not a blessing but a burden. She was a devoted church worker and pleased with her occupation, but it was not enough. "Something was missing," she explained. "I was moving ahead in my life, but I felt like I was standing still. There had to be more to life than just existing. I began to read writers like bell hooks and Renita Weems, and I discovered that to be a woman is more than I knew how. I decided to become more, to do whatever it took."

Revision by force: These sisters cling to their needs for others to define them. They are always looking for someone to rescue them. They will sink into quicksand of chaos until they realize that they are drowning and only they can save themselves.

Charlie Mae is such a woman. Her husband died fifteen years ago, leaving her widowed, alone, and helpless. "Prior to his death, my life seemed ideal," she recalled. "It dawned on me the morning after the funeral that I did not know anything about the insurance, the finances, or the debt. I was ignorant of my life. My husband handled all of the details. It was easy and fun to be taken care of at the time. I allowed myself not to know my own business. The bill collectors knocking at the door hastened me to learn about control and management of me. If they had not come, I would not have come to myself."

## Tending Your Garden

Are you ready for revision? A revised woman is like a gardener. Yes, a gardener. She tends her own garden. The garden is your life, your soul, your spirit. It's your values, your vagina. It's all of you. Whatever is growing there today was planted yesterday. Gardeners control their garden and not vice versa. They fiercely protect what is there. What will grow in your garden tomorrow is your decision today. Will it be leadership, courage, generosity? You are in control. This may feel uncomfortable, but you should get used to it. There is tremendous power in your hands. Use it to uncover the glory of God in you.

First, you clear the surface of your garden. Clearing is combing through what is there in your life. Take an inventory of you. Perhaps you can count your scars, bumps, and bruises. Recall your childhood friends, list your former sweethearts, or name the cities you have visited. Then ask yourself, "How am I better because of this?" Learn your surface, examine it, handle it. It may seem awkward at first. But this is a skill all women need. Combing through your self should give answers to the question of who you are.

Second, you pull the weeds from your garden. Weeds choke out the growth of valuable plants. They demand vast amounts of space and take up portions of your life. A number of weeds have flowers. Similarly, some of the mess in our lives is disguised as beauty. A weed is a weed. Remove them now. Weeding your garden means throwing out people, habits, and situations that obviously ought not to be there.

Third, you turn the soil. Unless the ground is turned, or aerated, there can be no planting and harvesting. Digging is a must. Digging reveals wounds—incest, abandonment, poverty, addiction, parental abuse, physical harm, illness, skin color. Digging reveals strengths—family, intelligence, persistence, faith and hope. Everything that surfaces is of value in determining who you are and who you shall be. You will decide what remains and what leaves. A superb tool for digging is a genogram. That's a fancy name for a detailed family tree.

Here is how one sister discovered that she needed it. Jane was stuck and could not move forward in life. She believed that she had "man problems." "My trouble is that I can't keep a man around," she said. "They always leave. I've tried everything to keep them—churching, cooking, cleaning, sexing. None of it worked. What is wrong with me?" Jane was on the verge of condemning herself for what seemed to be her problem. In actuality it was a generational problem of which she was the most recent beneficiary. She needed a clear view of her past to understand her present. Jane was reluctant to make a genogram.

"It seems like a list of work for nothing," she said. "Whatever is in my family tree needs to stay there. It is other people's problems, not mine."

Her tree revealed four generations of women who experienced divorce or separation in marriage. Jane saw a pattern that also engulfed her. She, too, had difficulty sustaining relationships because of a dominating relationship with her mother. Jane now understands that her challenges in relationships are linked to her historical relationship with her mother. She can refocus, redirect herself. There is no need to blame. Information empowers her to change. She can revise.

## Genograms

What is a genogram? It is a way of "drawing a family tree that records information about family members and their relationships over at least three generations."[6] It maps out how different family members are biologically, legally, and personally related to each other. A helpful book is *Genograms in Family Assessment* by Monica McGoldrick and Randy Gerson.

How can it help us? It enables us to see ourselves in a new way, ask questions, and make new connections. Family situations often repeat themselves. What happens in one generation will often repeat itself in the next.

What is the first step? Think about your answers to these questions: "What are the dates of births, marriages, separations, divorces, illnesses, and deaths in your family? What is your position within the birth order of your siblings? What are the occupations and educational levels of your family members? Do you know the current whereabouts of all living members?"[7]

1. *Getting started:* Use the following symbols to represent you and your family:

male □     female ○     deceased ⊠ ⊗

pregnancy ▽     stillbirth ⊠     miscarriage ●     abortion ✕

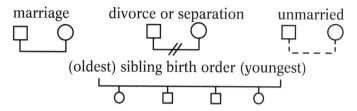

2. *Adding detailed information:* After you've drawn the family structure, begin adding the medical and other information about your family members, such as cancer, alcoholism, spouse battering.

3. *Family ties:* At this point most of your information is in place. Begin to describe the relationships between your family members. First think about your answers to these questions: Are there family members who do not speak to each other or who are extremely close? Who helps out when help is needed? Whom do family members confide in? How do you get along with your siblings? Has anyone been labeled the "sick," "bad," or "weak" one? Label the relationships using the following symbols:[8]

very close    ☐══○    close but conflicting ☐᷍᷍᷍᷍᷍᷍○
conflicting ☐᷍᷍᷍᷍○    close    ○══○
cut off       ☐┼┼○    distant ☐▪▪▪▪○

**More Gardening Work**

Fourth, you outline your garden. Where do you end? Where do you begin? Boundaries are essential to healthy gardens. Every strong woman relies on her boundaries to keep her balanced and aware of what's going on in her world. Your boundaries are powerful because they keep the good inside and keep the bad outside. The difference is that you decide. Remember, God made you an individual: "The very hairs on your head are numbered" (Luke 12:7). Here are a few signs of healthy boundaries:

• She keeps her own secrets.
• She knows what abuse feels like and will not accept it.
• She is able to say "no."

Fifth, you sow good seed into your garden. You must plant positive, edifying seeds deep inside yourself. Sow seeds into your own life. Don't depend on others to build you up. Others may sow good seeds, too, but don't wait on them. What you read sows. What you think sows. What you listen to sows. For example, when you wake up in the morning, sow seeds. Instead of saying "Good Lord, it's morning," say, "Good morning, Lord." Keep your mind on what is good. "Whatever is of good repute . . . let your mind dwell on these things" (Phil. 4:8).

Sixth, you must constantly cultivate. Nurture all that God has given you all the time. Cultivating your garden means encouraging yourself, monitoring yourself, listening to yourself, and guarding yourself. Cultivating demonstrates your love and pride in self. You must have the faith that God is working it out. Gardening must become a habitual way of life. It's your garden. Do not stop: You have officially started something. My dear, you are going places.

## Reflection Questions
1. Are you in need of a revision?
2. Can you make use of corrective love?
3. What specific steps can you take to "tend your garden"?

# 5. Sisterhood Future Style

"Entreat me not to leave you or to return from following you, for where you go, I will go, and where you live I will live. Your God will be my God, your people will be my people." (Ruth 1:16 NAS)

**As a teen,** I supposed that the supreme commitment flowing in Ruth 1:16 was between a man and a woman. Why? Who else was worth all of that pledging, swearing, and vowing but a man? It was pure church logic. If God made "man" in his image, then "man" was the only one worthy of a supreme relationship with me. I valued relationships with men and considered relationships with women as chump change. I learned well. All of those years in Sunday school did not go to waste. I was a star pupil of my religious regime. I was primed and prepared to make pleasing men my priority. Innocently and automatically I built up the good ol' boy system at the expense of sisterhood. They had the power. I wanted it and acted accordingly. Friendships with women were a perfunctory stepping stone.

I became proficient in devaluing girls and women. Instinctively I downplayed a "her" for a "him." I graduated from a women's college, where sisterhood was the expectation. Yet true relationships were elusive. Sisterhood was not automatic in a male-dominated society, even if the school was all female. Intimidation, jealousy, and competition were my instant responses to a campus teeming with smart, pretty, congenial female students.

As a freshman I drowned in jealousy. I'd size up every student I encountered and rapidly categorize her as either better than me, smarter than me, prettier than me, or less than me. The more she had—in grades, looks, boyfriends, sorority affiliation—the more I despised her. The less she had, the more I liked her. It was a sick method of "handling" women; after all they were just stepping stones.

Years later, as with the apostle Paul, the scales of ignorance fell from my eyes. It was a happy day when I read the Bible myself and comprehended the value of women's relationships with each other. Our stories of authentic union are told in the Scriptures. Often overlooked and rarely preached, they are there. Sister relationships are valuable and worth the effort and investment. There were the women who accompanied Jesus as he ministered. Surely they saw their womanhood as an asset. Luke 8:2 tells us about these women ". . . who had been healed of evil spirits and infirmities; Mary, called Magdalene, from whom seven demons had gone out, and Joanna, the wife of Chuza, Herod's steward, and Susanna, and many others, who provided for them out of their means."

Under the lens of New Faith we magnify this scene and seek to replicate it. We can learn from this sisterhood what Jesus wanted for women—to commit themselves to following him and develop unity, even if that means temporarily leaving the men in our lives. (Sisterhood is not anti-male or anti-marriage, but if your man loves Jesus too, he will understand and accept what Jesus is doing in your life.) Jesus was their common denominator. They built their relationships with each other through him. He is the superglue for sisterhood. Nothing else can hold us tightly together. We can find peace here. He is our shelter from our divisive habits.

If we can get real, we will admit that often we are less like the women who were with Jesus and more like the women who were without Jesus. Many of us Bible-toting, hymn-singing church women bear the marks of matriculation in male-dominated churches. The life of the dominated among the dominators is violent. This violence is not with guns but with attitudes, prejudice, and most lethal—the tongue. Bell hooks calls it "woman-hating."[1] It is a learned behavior. As hooks says,

> Male supremacist ideology encourages women to believe we are valueless and obtain value only by relating to or bonding with men. We are taught that our relationships with one another diminish rather than enrich our experience.[2]

Throughout Christendom women are slicing and dicing each other to shreds in the name of Jesus. We strike out at each other because there is no one else we can affect. Our powerlessness in the church hierarchy guarantees that we strike each other. With the Bible in one hand and the phone in the other we are skilled in reducing women with ridicule during conversations after church. After we have removed our holy hats and sanctified shoes, it begins: "Who does she think she is? What was she trying to prove? She makes me ill. If she's heading the committee, I am getting off." This is what I call pseudo-sisterhood. It is a fraction of, a portion of, a segment of real sisterhood.

Mary and Martha are prime examples of the biblical pseudo-sisterhood. In Luke 10:3 Martha realizes that Mary is moving forward and wants Jesus to help force Mary back in control. "Tell her to help me," demands Martha. In other words, "make her act like me. I won't permit her to have thoughts unlike mine. She must live within my world, with my cramped mindset. Otherwise she is conceited and uppity and thinks that she is hot stuff."

There is a bit of Martha in all of us. I will be the first to confess that it became comfortable there in the limitations erected by sexism to keep us in our places. Moving beyond the limitations made me envious and anxious. It felt natural for men to have us where they wanted us as women. If they keep us fighting over the crumbs, the pie is left for them. In this new century, women will be stepping beyond even more established boundaries, and claiming new territories. Toni Morrison was accurate when she wrote, "I am alarmed by the violence that women do to each other: professional violence, competitive violence, emotional violence. I am alarmed by the willingness of women to enslave other women. I am alarmed by a growing absence of decency on the killing floor of professional women's worlds."[3]

## The Walls That Divide

In my research on African American church women, I have discovered four issues that divide us: isolation, skin color, hair texture, and physical traits. Isolation is one of our greatest threats, say sociologists. The stress of life isolates or locks us away from contact with other women. For example, after work you come home, help the kids with homework, feed them, and dash off to choir rehearsal, while keeping your weekend job till Christmas and hosting your in-laws till their home is remodeled. And all the while your fibroids are flaring up and you think that your husband is going Muslim. The chaos that swirls around us will cut us off from others. It will suck us into the center of itself.

Do you know what happens to women who exist without healthy contact with positive sisters? They are bound for antagonism, depression, hopelessness, and hostility, because there are no positive women for them to reflect. Instead they may gravitate to negative ones. They will stumble into a desertlike experience and succumb to a drought of the soul and spirit.

I've seen parched, withered sisters drag into church, looking as well-groomed as possible on the outside, but dry and lifeless on the inside. Try to smile at them and start a conversation, and your head may be handed back to you. New Faith ends isolation. We have the same parent. Our destiny is tied in the same garment. The 1990s saw the "Million Woman March." The 2000s will see the multimillion women tearing down the walls that divide us.

The pursuit of men divides us. (Men are truly gracious gifts from God. Our pursuit or preoccupation with possessing them turns us into rivals.) He can be as handsome as chocolate velvet or ugly as a stick, a wealthy businessman or broke as a beggar, but to many women the value of his maleness is beyond measure. In the church community having a man in worship is about as important as bringing your Bible. He is a man, and many a sister will do just about anything to get him and to keep him. It matters not that he is engaged to, married to, or dating another sister. In fact, some sisters make a habit of stealing somebody else's man. This is disrespect of the self, the sister, and God. For example, Tanya is the choir director at her church for two reasons: she has a degree in music, and she gets first dibs on the men who join the choir. "Yes, I prefer the married ones," she said. "That's just my tastes. Deal with it. God knows my weakness and forgives me."

The texture of our hair divides us. Ever since Madame C. J. Walker became a millionaire manufacturer of hair concoctions, we have worried ourselves silly about our hair. Hair means a lot to us, maybe too much. Whether we braid it, twist it, weave it, perm it, shave it off, or dread it, there are ramifications accompanying the choice of style. Some sisters feel that nappy hair is low-class and shun short-haired, "fuzzy" women. "I can't deal with the happy, nappy look. It brings the race down. She won't be a part of this committee," said one woman. One historical motto forbids sons from bringing home to momma women with hair that was not "silky." "If she can't use my comb, don't bring her home" goes the adage.

The color of our skin divides us. There is a "pigmentoc-racy" in America that gives favor to those with the lighter hues of skin.[4] In this prejudiced society a compliment to ebony-hued sisters is, "You are a pretty Black girl." The message is that although you are dark, you somehow possess pretty (Anglo) features. Thus you have been redeemed. The light-skinned girls with long hair were presumed "automatics" for dances and parties and had the access to the cutest boys. It was as if all they had to do was show up and they were the winners of it all.

Our physical features divide us. Wide lips, noses, and feet are a source of pride or embarrassment. Cruel names like "soup cooler" lips and "bull nose" flow freely. An especially ubiquitous trait is sizeable hips. This is truly a Black woman trait that we cannot shake off.

New Faith won't let our locks divide us. It reminds us that Jesus had hair like "lambs' wool." New Faith gives us an appreciation of the rainbow of women from blue-black to snow-white. New Faith issues a theology that reveres what God has given us—our skin, our hair, and our butts. Surely God must be saying something to us or through us with our physiology. There is an abundance here—no limits, no contractions, no rationing—an ample supply. This is a good thing. New Faith forces us to embrace every woman as our sister, because we cannot have a future without each other. No longer are we competition. Our faith in God is more powerful than our outer characteristics. New Faith tells us where we went wrong and with the snap of a hand points the right way to go. Does it matter if her skin is as dark as charcoal or fair as the snow? Does it matter if her nose is as wide as a freeway or narrow like a rural pathway? Why do we dwell on the outside, my sister? Your potential friend is not composed of nostrils or melanin but the soul. We must have soul sisters. Our souls require each other.

Yes, a soul sister. There is so much complex beauty contained within us. The soul of your sister can be a lifeline; it can bring you from the brink of isolation or swoop you from the pit of suicide. The sound of a voice you know can revive you. Who else knows about our historical ash, the sizzle of the straightening combs, and the funk of chitterlings taking over the house one room at a time? Who else can pop gum, do a fierce Whitney Houston imitation, and braid your hair? Who else can get the "spirit" in church, holy dance all across the front sanctuary, and never muss that too-tough "do"? There is no mistaking a sister. We must cultivate an adoration for us and be our own safe places and nesting niches. We can no longer afford to be at odds over anything—a man, a job, or money.

## No Enemies Here!

In the name of New Faith, I call a cease-fire. Desist from all catfights, name-calling, finger-pointing. New Faith declares that we are all on the same side: There are no enemies here. New Faith taught me that if I love Jesus, then I love me, and I must love my sister. It is a natural progression of love. Now I know that women must be about the business of alliances, coalitions, and clusters with women for our own good. New Faith instructs us to re-create sisterhood for these new times. This time our connection is not based on common oppression but on common victory. New Faith sets the establishment of sisterhood high on our list of requirements for survival in this new millennium. Before we can start pledging like Ruth and Naomi, we take these steps:

1. Exhale any negatives. Forgive her for whatever someone else did or did not do. This sister does not deserve yesterday's anger.
2. Rehearse in your mind good deeds by our foremothers— Clara Hale, Rosa Parks, Fannie Lou Hamer. This sister you are meeting may be the next heroine.

3. Alter your attitude. Hold your neck, if need be, to keep it from working involuntarily. Try not to jump to conclusions when you think someone is disrespecting you. This sister may base her reaction on yours. Be the role model for her to reflect on.

4. Speak to each other in love. Monitor the tone of your voice. Shower this sister in the melody of your voice.

5. Smile. Make eye contact. This sister is you. Don't you deserve the best?

6. Create your own safe places. Sponsor events in your home that give women a place to vent and voice. Create new ministries in your church to nurture the souls of women. This sister may need a harbor in the storm.

7. Pray for each other. Lift up each other daily in your talk with God. Intercede for women in turmoil—those who are homeless, without money, without freedom and those with all the material goods but no connection with God. Believe that God can make a way out of no way. Sisters everywhere need your prayers.

With your sisters locked in step with you, nothing is impossible. A chorus of us—heads thrown back, voices piercing the sky—is awesome. Your sisters will keep you marching. Their energy will propel you forward when you are weary. Their shoulders will prop you up when you are sad. Their eyes are your spotlights. Their backs are your bridge.

## Reflection Questions

1. What has male supremacy done to sisterhood?
2. Is there any Martha in you?
3. What divides you from other women?

# 6. Rocking the Cradle and the World

"Her children rise up and call her blessed." (Prov. 28:31 NAS)

**W**hen **New Faith** merges with motherhood there is a new message: Motherhood is a revolutionary act. Whether we have given birth through our loins, or we care for someone else's kids, all women are revolutionaries. We can create, host, and give birth with our bodies. Our wombs populate the globe. We possess reproductive spirits. That is a power that defies the vocabulary.

This is not a lesson taught in Sunday school in the church I grew up in. If I had been taught that my ability to mother was a trait of God, I would have been a different girl. How so? Perhaps I would have been vaccinated from the temptation to have sex before marriage or made proud that my body contained God-like reproducing equipment. Instead I scorned my body's "monthly plague."

Motherhood—powerful motherhood—is a religious issue because it highlights commonalities between women and God. New Faith says we should brag about it. The godfather of soul, James Brown, sang a song I'll never forget: "Papa's Got a Brand-New Bag." He was gleeful that he possessed a newness and bragged to the world that he was changed. Momma has got a brand-new bag too; she's had it all along. New Faith says, Seize the bag and tell the world to watch out.

## Black Mothers

Motherhood for us has been a complex bag. Ever since African feet touched the shores of America, Black mothers have been forced to live complex lives of bitterness and blessing, of satisfaction and sorrow. Much of this revolved around God. Something within us could not be held down, and our strong maternal instincts gave us clout with historical dimensions. As a result many of us have been nurturing and mothering just about everything and everybody—friend or foe—since then.

In the 1800s in genteel circles, some Black women were the highly esteemed mammies for massa and those in the Anglo households. Revered and feared by all of the ruling owners, some mammies were actually preferred over biological mothers. In the cruel surroundings of slavery's woodsheds, fields, and barns, some of us were "breeder women," forced pregnant with various men's children every year, only to have the child sold away.

Today we remain complex. We are competent Big Momma, Ma'Dear, Ma. We are the no-nonsense sisters who rule with an iron hand and cuddle with deep-dish peach cobbler. We are also the irresponsible females who ditch our kids for the attention of any man or who give birth solely to entrap a man.

Church mothers are renowned for their child-care techniques. Care for children is often a paramount characteristic, coupled with the desire not to be embarrassed by children in public. Church mothers can be divided into at least three categories. There are usually older mothers who offer candy to pacify rowdy children. Their purses are stuffed with candies to dispense. Their job, as they see it, is to keep the kids' mouths chock-full of treats.

There are the radar mothers. Such a mother may be in the choir loft heartily singing soprano, yet she instinctually knows when her child, sitting in the sanctuary, is misbehaving. With the skill of military radar, she locks onto her target and launches a series of facial gyrations that shock the child back into line. Then there are the "other mothers" in church—women who are not even related to the child but sense their community connection and have no problem rushing forth to corral and correct any wayward child within their range.

The connection between the Black church and Black women, particularly mothers, cannot be stressed enough. The terms *Black mother* and *Black church* are synonymous. The valid question can be asked, "Can you have one without the other?" As has been discussed in earlier chapters, the strong affinity between the church and mothers began in slavery.

Throughout all of history, the church has been the support system for Black mothers. This also includes women who are pregnant out of wedlock. Whether their pregnancy is overlooked or publicly scorned, that mother eventually has a place in the church community. The church has always been a reliable place for spiritual, social, and emotional refuge. Specifically, in the time of slavery, "God and religion fulfilled some very basic needs that could not be fulfilled by the slave community or the black man. Thus the slave narratives often portray black mothers exhibiting a vigorous spiritual self-confidence even though their sexuality has been completely brutalized and exploited by white men of every social class. . . . They endured because, as one slave mother taught her daughter, they believed there was 'nobody in the wide world to look at but God.'"[1]

Although church was the "savior" for Black mothers, it also held the realized threat of power loss. The sexism woven into the very fabric of the church hemmed Black mothers into power-draining corners and pockets. They were pigeonholed ever so sweetly into second-class positions, as the real authority was never given to them but was passed over their heads. According to historical record, after slavery came the "business of transferring power to the males in the ex-slave community to create a more stable patriarchal model. There are indications that even before the Civil War the institutionalization of black religion . . . carried with it the subordination and oppression of women."[2]

It can be assumed that the wrongdoing of sexism did not compare to the horrors of slavery. The women may not have desired to grapple with their men for control. But, for those few women who dared step forward, trouble came. Jarena Lee, one of the earliest preachers in the African Methodist Episcopal Church, recounted how she was treated by founder Richard Allen and other male preachers:

> I went to see the preacher in charge of the African society . . . the Rev. Richard Allen . . . to tell him that I felt it my duty to preach the gospel. . . . He then replied that a Mrs. Cook, a Methodist lady, had also some time before requested the same privilege. But as to preaching, he said that our Discipline knew nothing at all about it—that it did not call for women preachers.[3]

Another crucial point that springs from the slavery context focuses on the relationships between mothers and their children's father. Slavery's harshness meant that families could be divided at any point.

> . . . It is perhaps not too far-fetched to suggest that in their struggle to survive and nurture their own, many antebellum black mothers often had as their helpmate not the black man but black religion. The black man was the lowest in authority in the slave system. Hence

black mothers and nurturers depended upon their
religion for psychological and emotional support.[4]
Men, and therefore fathers, may have been a luxury to the
slave women. This trouble lingers on today.

## Reclaiming Motherhood

Our mothers did the best that they could, but they were
not privy to power, and they could not give it to us. Motherhood is diluted. As it exists today, this institution is a
comatose giant. The effects of the past can be seen in
three areas.

Dilution is seen in the traditional tributes to mothers.
Churches across the nation note Mother's Day as the
Sunday in May to affix a plastic flower to women's dresses, sing a few hymns, and have us grin through a canned
sermon on Proverbs 31. We are perfunctorily lauded,
whether our kids are drug fiends or doctoral candidates,
and whether we are doting guardians or hapless crack-
heads. And our children usually do thank us, but for
what—cooking, cleaning, jail bond? We should be pass-
ing more to them.

A second sign of power loss is the state of our children.
Statistically there are more young African American men
languishing in prisons or lounging on street corners in
gangs than there are in college or in productive pursuits.
The figures tell us that more teenage girls are sexually
active and/or mothers than ever in the history of our people. These young people were reared by somebody, right?
The squandered lives of our children damage our
résumés. This situation is below our capability.

A third sign is the estrangement between mothers and
fathers. There has been an unwritten rule that most
women can make it without the father of her children. A
casual resignation automatically rises if the father does
not live up to the expectations of support or even interest
in the child. The father can be demoted from responsibil-

ity to the title "just my baby's daddy." And as a result men have descended to meet those low expectations.

New Faith reminds us that mothers mold and shape the minds of their children by their actions and words. What are we teaching? What we allow, we teach. Our children see us accepting second best, tolerating oppression, bowing down to foolishness. They learn to understand that this is what we deserve. In this new millennium much more will be demanded and exacted from our children. Will we prepare them for success or slaughter? Children are crying out for safety in this spinning, maddening world. They need consistency and grounding. They need New Faith mothers who know God, themselves, and what children need. "Mothering thus requires an ability and willingness to maintain traditions while reshaping them for future generations—discarding that which is not nurturing and upholding while incorporating that which is."[5]

New Faith refuses to surrender our power to sexism. We can begin to reclaim it with a womanist review of the Word of God. Hagar is a mother in the Scriptures often cited because we all have been exploited and disenfranchised by the oppressor, but blessed and empowered by God. "Her importance in the African American folk tradition is secured by the affirmation that 'we are Aunt Hagar's children.'"[6]

Her enslavement and abuse at the hands of Abram and Sari are not the focus today. This plight has a blessed ending. Hagar resists evil by running away in the first instance and by weeping aloud in the wilderness in the second. What womanist theologian Cheryl Sanders highlights is Hagar's unparalleled act of "naming God." Once God reveals that her child Ishmael (which means "God hears") will have numerous offspring, she responds to God with "You are El-Roi: for she said . . . Have I seen God and remained alive after seeing him?"[7] Sanders wants us to see the connection between Hagar's son, Ishmael, and God. She writes, "If there is a miraculous intervention here, it is not providing water in the desert, but rather it is the blessing of insight and awareness. It is God showing the mother that the very thing she needs for her family's survival is within her reach."[8]

Mary is another mother in the Bible who offers us insight into the style of powerful motherhood. As a young Hebrew girl, Mary knew the limitations placed on her life because of her gender. The angel of the Lord came to her with good news and glad tidings: "Hail, O favored one, the Lord is with you!" (Luke 1:28). Mary was disturbed by the message: ". . . She was greatly troubled at the saying, and considered what kind of greeting this might be" (Luke 1:29). It was more than she could ever hope for. The sexism that clouded her life served as blinders on her eyes and a governor of her aspirations.

Certainly Mary's plight describes many African American Christian women—able, equipped, and empowered to do a great work for God, yet bound by sexism. What is crucial to note here is that Mary eventually understood that when God plants a ministry, vision, plan, or program in your spirit, nothing and no one can deter it. Mary replied to the angel, "How can this be?" The angel told her, "For with God nothing will be impossible" (Luke 1:37). From that point Mary went forth to indeed complete a great work for God, with God. It is important to note that she was assisted by her husband, not authorized. He too realized the greatness of God and his role as supporting God in her life. This is a vibrant vision for the relationship of mothers and fathers.

## A Brand-New Bag

There are numerous areas where New Faith women can enhance their motherhood. Space permits only a partial list to be offered: embracing lifelong learning, making authentic strides toward respectful communication with their children, and, most important, straight talk about sex.

Motherhood must be a continual learning experience. There is an abundance of innovative information in our society that we don't know that can help us. It is unfortunate that sometimes the new information that can illuminate us only intimidates us. That was my experience once when parenting classes were offered to a group of church mothers. "Don't tell me how to raise my kids!" said one mother. "I think I know what's right and wrong for my family," said another. These statements indicate a high level of resistance to learning and a probable failure to be the best moms they could have been. New Faith encourages mothers to always seek to grow as long as they are living.

Communicating with our children is the second concern for mothers. A common sound overheard in grocery stores, shopping malls, and even the church vestibule is a mother verbally lashing her child. "You are so stupid! What's wrong with you? I'll knock you into next week" are statements flung in the ears of admittedly misbehaving children. The berating is enough to stunt the child's self-esteem and propel the mother into a cycle of harassing. New Faith encourages mothers to speak to their children with dignity, lower the tones of their voices, and eliminate the violent threats. Screaming and losing control are not virtues of motherhood.

Church women have been long on folk sayings ("Don't let me hear about your dress being up and your panties being down") and short on facts. Fear tactics about sex are not effective. Our children need comprehensive sexuality education. It is not enough to know about the birds and the bees. They should also know how to prevent little bees from reproducing and how to protect themselves from sexually transmitted diseases.

In a group of women discussing their girlhood and the impact of sex education or lack of such information from their mothers, a predictable pattern emerged. "If I even brought up the subject I was punished," said one woman. "She thought I was a 'bad girl.'" "My mother wanted to talk to me about it, I know she did," said another one, "but she did not know how."

I suggest that the most crucial act for mothers is to initiate and maintain dialogue on the topic of sex with their children. Ignorance in this area cripples our children. New Faith moms understand that the socialization differences between boys and girls hurl them into headlong collisions. We understand that programming them in opposite directions perpetuates the scrimmages and sniping between them. Moms can rear them with equality— same curfews, dating rules, off-limits places. Let's advise both genders to abstain from sex, and if they cannot, advise them to make use of condoms. If pregnancy ensues, let's hold both genders accountable.

Things I wish mom had told me:

1. You are beautiful as you are. Spend time alone marveling at yourself. Learn every space of your flesh; touch your breasts, hips, vagina. They are all yours.

2. You have the right to build and enforce your own boundaries. What you don't want done to you, don't allow. If someone makes you uncomfortable, leave. If someone pesters you, call the cops.

3. Learn to say no. Speak up for yourself. Learning to say no keeps you true to yourself.

4. Speak with confidence. Look people in the eye when you speak. Your voice sets the tone, and your eyes walk into their souls.

5. Be sexually responsible. Sex is a gift for marriage. Remain a virgin as long as possible. Virgins have fun, too. You are a sexual being. That's the way God made

you. Your body will develop and mature so it can bring forth life and offer you sexual pleasure. Both of these are good, but they have tremendous consequences. It's up to you to make the choice that reflects who you are—beautiful, smart, and powerful.

Mothers, we are revolutionaries. We give birth, we change things. The power of God is within our reach. Our momentum is building. Let's keep on moving. There is more ahead.

## Reflection Questions

1. What images of Black church mothers do you have?
2. How does Hagar help us to understand our past and future as mothers?
3. What do you wish your mother had told you (or warned you) about?

# 7. Brothers

"Barak said to her, 'If you will go with me, I will go; but if you will not go with me, I will not go.'" (Judges 4:8)

**R**eading about the biblical, God-ordained partnership between a fierce male warrior, Barak, and a prestigious female judge, Deborah, always puts a huge grin on my face. This passage proves once and for all that men and women can work together without sexual harassment, jockeying for top position, or clinging to gender stereotypes. We belong side by side. As a pastor, mother, wife, and woman, I've yearned for the day when we who are the image of God could put our agendas aside and let God use us freely. Then it wouldn't matter whose name was first, who received credit, or who led the event. Men and women were created to live in harmony. We were fashioned by the same God, for the same purpose: to worship and serve God.

Strong women in concert with strong men are the fruit of New Faith. It is the destiny of a people who believe that God can conquer anything. Our common history makes us brothers and sisters first. The irrepressible message for this millennium is that anything that divides or stratifies us is *un*godly. There is a primacy in our sibling nature. Here men and women view God as parent and each other as brother and sister.

Sisters, as we strive toward this goal, we understand that our strength comes from God rather than the presence of a man. We understand that we must be developed, refined, and mature prior to entering partnerships with brothers on any level. A weakened woman (one who is not developed, refined, and mature) is a victim. For such women any level of relationship with a man can lead to personal ruin. It is unwise to place oneself in such predicaments. New Faith prepares women to be sisters. Realistically we need lessons like those in chapters 1 through 4 of this book to move us to the point of internal strength to interact positively. If we have mastered those lessons, we will be ready. If we have not, we will not be ready. Our insecurities, hurts, and baggage will color all men the enemies, losers, dogs, and worse.

## The Bible and Gender Wars

New Faith declares that men are good. They are a part of God's design for the world. Like us, they are created in the image of God. According to Genesis 1:27: "So God created them in his own image, in the image of God he created them; male and female" (NRSV). This Scripture passage gives balance to the skewed perceptions running rampant among us. We are too important to each other to squabble over control.

If I were to begin a theology of men, as in "male gender," the theology would spring from a man's relationship with his surroundings—the elements, the animals, and the women. When God scooped up clay and blew breath into him, giving him life, God made a marvelous miracle called man. Men play a co-central role in the universe that will never be denied, denigrated, or destabilized. God called him "good," and so do I. Men are irreplaceable and one-of-a-kind; they are not the enemy. If they were, God would not have created us both in God's image or placed us together in the garden. In God's design, men function with us as blessings to each other.

We were designed for partnership first. Unfortunately, the patriarchal history of the church has not endorsed partnerships and well-balanced perceptions between men and women. Some believe it is unscriptural for women and men to work together as equals. As a result, there is a silent and sometimes not-so-silent war. To date, the church is responsible for the gender divisions. Men and women have been religiously programmed to be at each other's throats.

I speculate that there are a handful of biblical texts used to keep men and women at odds. These texts come from letters attributed to the apostle Paul and are a sticking point in most discussions about men and women:

- "I do not permit a woman to teach or have authority over a man. She must be silent" (1 Tim. 2:12).
- "Women should remain silent in the church. They are not allowed to speak, but must be in submission as the Law says" (1 Cor. 14:34).

What did Paul really mean? There are inconsistencies in his writings, and scholars dispute whether all the opinions expressed come from Paul himself. The Paul who wrote women into dominated silence and powerlessness also wrote about humanity's oneness in Christ. The scriptural texts of Galatians 3:28, "There is neither Jew nor Greek, . . . there is neither male nor female; for you are all one in Christ Jesus," as well as Colossians 3:11, "but Christ is all, and in all," point toward equality of genders. Noted preacher and teacher Dr. Vashti M. McKenzie suggests that there were vast differences in Paul's thought and writings. "It is ironic that in these two pericopes and others, Paul is seen issuing a call for a new humanity, united and reconciled. Paul affirms inclusiveness that does not exclude female leadership. The divisive notions of superiority and inferiority based on class, race and social and sexual grounds come under attack. They find no validity in Christ."[1]

Dr. McKenzie further suggests: "Paul is portrayed as a wimp, changing his mind to fit his audience. Or perhaps he grew egalitarian between 1 Corinthians and Galatians. Or perhaps later editors projected patriarchal perspectives on what some viewed as radical counterculture behavior."[2] She finally suggests, "If women were to keep silent, did he mean that Priscilla should have kept her mouth closed rather than correct Apollos? Or that Mary Magdalene should have kept her mouth closed rather than tell the disciples who did not come early to the tombs?"[3]

Extensive damage has been done to God's sibling plan by this mindset. To further understand the impact, let's look more closely at church experiences. In some churches the notion that men are supposed to be "over" women is so ingrained that it is not ever possible to work as equals on anything. There is no parity of thought or action. Here's what I mean. Dawn and Stephen both sing in the choir. They have been members of the church for ten years each. When they volunteered to coordinate the choir's fundraiser, trouble arose due to religious gender expectations. Stephen expected to be the leader of the team. He expected Dawn to agree with his plans and carry out the menial tasks like typing, faxing, and phoning, while he made the presentations to the congregation, met with the pastor, and made decisions. After all, he was the man. "I thought it was understood," he said. "Men lead. Women follow. It's biblical; it's scriptural. Case closed." Dawn, unaware that she was to let him lead, displayed her authority. "I've got a brain, common sense, plus a college degree. Why should I stop thinking because a man walks in the room?" There was friction all the way, and ultimately the fundraiser was poorly planned and poorly attended.

This gender war maims the spirits of many, especially young girls. An informal assembly had gathered in the fellowship hall to hear the plans for the annual barbecue. A request came forth from the speaker for persons to serve in leadership roles. Although I was just twelve, my hand shot up with eagerness. I thought, "Sure, I can do that." My volunteerism was met with a rejection. "Let the men lead, honey," she gently chided me. She was Mother McClain, an elderly sister of the church. Regarded as the "mother" of the church, she was admired and revered by all. Mother McClain did not know me. I was a visitor at her church, but she knew I was getting too close to the power source, and I had to get back. Her firm grip on my shoulder told me to stop approaching leadership or standing too tall when men were around. It was their job to shine, not ours.

This was a bitter lesson. I was a child and did not understand the biblical differences between boys and girls. I thought we were all one in Christ Jesus. Her words entered my ears and flowed directly into my belly, where they churned and soured like a poison. I knew that girls and boys grow up on the playground as equals. They run, jump, romp, and laugh all the same. At some point in their maturation process the girls are supposed to know that it is no longer acceptable for them to strive beside or sometimes in front of the boys. Who decides this? Is there some committee?

## Keys to the Conflict

Psychologist Jean Baker Miller offers important keys to unlocking these conflicts and other entanglements of women and men. She labels the basic relationships between men and women in general as "dominant-subordinate." Black men are the dominants; Black women are the subordinates. The Black church is a supreme case study for the "dominant-subordinate" framework in action.[4] This dominant-subordinate framework is employed in varying degrees—sometimes intentionally. Male leadership clearly defines areas where women are forbidden to serve, such as communion stewards, finance committees, deacons, trustee boards, and pastors. Women are barred from these posts because of a biblical understanding based on the maleness of God and of Jesus. Another form of the dominant-subordinate framework is the monitoring of women's attire. In some churches, women are forbidden to wear pants and are required to wear pantyhose to be admitted to the sanctuary.

At other times, the framework is subtle. The ear is trained with noninclusive language in the church that does not reveal the female side of God. The eye is trained by a pulpit filled with men who teach the lesson that church is a place for men to lead and for women to follow.

Baker Miller further suggests that dominant groups:

- tend to be destructive of subordinate groups, label them defective, impede their development and block their freedom of expression and action
- hold themselves as the model for "normal" human relationships
- generally do not like to be told about or even quietly reminded of the existence of inequality
- prefer to avoid conflict and see any questioning of the "normal" situation as threatening
- usually define one or more acceptable roles for subdominants. These "acceptable" roles typically involve providing services that no dominant group wants to provide for itself. The functions that the dominant group wants to perform are carefully guarded and closed to the subordinates. Dominants tell subordinates

that they are unable to perform the preferred roles. Their incapacities are ascribed to innate defects or deficiency of mind or body, therefore immutable and impossible to change.[5]

In the heat of this gender war, once again we are forced to choose between loyalty to God, dignity to self, and a desire for our men. We want our men in our lives, but at what cost? For the most part it is easier for some women to go along with their men than fight this age-old, Bible-based war. Our silence buys us a form of pseudo-sibling existence. We can utilize the brother and sister connection as long as we act accordingly.

The suppression is seen in our lives outside the church, too. It has been said that "racism in this country has given black men a strange edge over their sisters. Black women have been taught that it is OK to get angry when it comes to white people and racism, and to express that anger openly. At the same time we are taught that it is wrong, dead wrong to be angry and vocal about black men and sexism."[6]

There is a certain penalty for Black women who speak anything "that would remotely hold Black men accountable for their behavior."[7] When men are confronted, corrected, and challenged by women, the women are vilified—à la Anita Hill, Desiree Washington, C. Delores Tucker. Women who do speak up may be labeled anti-Black, anti-struggle, anti-Black male, sell-out, handkerchief-wearing house nigger, castrating woman, or bitch.[8] The thinking is that surely a sister who corrects a Black man has been bought out by the White man for the express purposes of bringing down yet another brother.

## Sisters and Brothers in Truth

New Faith detests the historical muzzle on the lips of African American Christian women and removes it. New Faith reminds us that we must always speak the truth.

Silence in the presence of evil is counter our faith in Christ, who did not shrink back from evil. I remember the day that I spoke up.

"Why are the men out front styling and profiling and the women are back here in the kitchen sweating our hair out?" I asked one day out of the blue. The kitchen hummed with sisters eager to work for the cause and never to question.

My speaking up and out was not an act of racial treason but a faith move. "Acknowledging sexism of Black men does not mean that we become man-haters or necessarily eliminate them from our lives. What it does mean is that we must struggle for a different basis of understanding with them."[9] One analysis of why Black women do not identify sexism in black men is "because they fear it could lead to greater victimization."[10] Additionally others suggest that many Black women have not joined public movements against sexism because they have not seen one that works.[11]

New Faith also offers a method and means of reclaiming our sibling relationships. I suggest that New Faith works because it relies on God, and God does not fail. It gives the oppressed and the oppressor a means to unite for a common goal. It is a way out of no way for brothers and sisters trapped in a legacy of divisive tradition.

Second, New Faith helps men to understand the privilege of sexism. In the same way that Anglos understand and admit their access to White privilege, our men must do the same. This is not a hurtful or harmful act. The truth sets us free. "All men support and perpetuate sexism and sexist oppression in one form or another. Like women, men have been socialized to passively accept sexist ideology. While they need not blame themselves for accepting sexism, they must assume responsibility for eliminating it."[12]

In the church world, we understand that all men have this privilege whether they are the janitor or the pastor. Maleness conveys instant power, prestige, and position. It may be difficult for our men to confess this privilege because the church-based power is sometimes the only status they own. They may understand the misinterpreted Scripture as their solitary key to status. They may wonder what they benefit by releasing their one sure tool.

Here is a probable scenario.

> The poor or working class man who has been social-ized via sexist ideology to believe that there are privi-leges and powers he should possess solely because he is a man often finds that few if any of these benefits are automatically bestowed on him in life. More than any other male group in the United States, he is constant-ly concerned about the contradiction between the notion of masculinity he was taught and his inability to live up to that notion. He is usually hurt—emo-tionally scarred because he does not have the privilege or power society has taught him that "real" men should possess. Alienated, frustrated and pissed off, he may attack, abuse and oppress an individual woman or women, but he is not reaping positive benefits from his support and perpetuation of sexist ideology.[13]

Men do not benefit from the gender war. Women do not benefit. The church and the community do not benefit. Why continue? Christian African American men need the sibling relationships as much as we do. Our community cries out for unity and peace with other races. Let's begin at home.

We are in crisis, but it was crisis that brought Deborah and Barak together. Jabin, the cruel Canaanite leader who possessed nine hundred iron chariots, had opposed the Israelites for twenty years. The Israelites cried to the Lord for help. God sent Deborah—a woman. She held the dual function of prophet and judge. "In the book of Judges the function of the judging role seems to be twofold. Judges were sometimes those to whom cases or disputes could be brought for decision; in other instances they were charismatic leaders raised up by God, usually for military emergency."[14] Deborah was also a prophet, as were three other Old Testament women, Miriam (Ex. 15:20), Huldah (2 Kings 22:14), and Noadiah (Neh. 6:4). "The most frequent responsibility of a prophet was to convey something of God's will or plan to the people."[15]

In verse 6 Deborah summons Barak and informs him of God's plans, which include battle, an enemy, and certain victory. Barak came and listened. As a brother and a comrade in the struggle, he willingly heard what God said through her. He respected her and the urgency of the national threat. Her leadership position in the community was understood. It is curious to some biblical commentators that he was unwilling to go into battle without her. Specifically, he beseeches her into a partnership on which hinges the fate of their people. "If you will go with me, I will go; but if you will not go with me, I will not go." As a partner with a man, Deborah was a woman of authority. Her authority came from God; it created in her an influence that Barak surrendered to willingly.

One scholar has said, "It seems clear, however, that Barak thought Deborah's presence would in some way assure the promised victory."[16] Was he weak because he asked a woman for help? No! The traditional male-dominated framework would insist that a man should be able to handle battle on his own. And that a woman's place is not in battle but in the home, tending to the family. New Faith concurs that Barak's position of partnering with Deborah was best. He must have known that in battle two are stronger than one, that women are valuable to the struggle, and that God's validation of Deborah was irrefutable and therefore should be respected. The battle concludes as Deborah prophesied it would. The Israelites were victorious, and a woman, Jael, ultimately killed the general.

Chapter 5 of Judges contains "Deborah's Song," in which both Deborah and Barak celebrate the victory. In candor, I will say that war, spoilage, and murder are not admirable themes. Yet the fact that Deborah and Barak conquered together is paramount for this discussion. These Old Testament high-profilers singlehandedly shift the male–female paradigm. They challenge conservative Christian thought, which locks men and women into gender-specific roles. They challenge biblical literalists who declare that women have access to diminished power in the presence of men.

Deborah and Barak illustrate this millennium's required relationship. Deborah is a New Faith woman because she brothers Barak. Brothering is an act of strong women. It supports, endorses, and helps a man without harming self. It is the first level of relationship that women should have with men. Women, we must communicate clearly with our brothers. Deborah got right to the point. Sometimes we send conflicting messages. Sometimes we are overwhelmed and intimidated by men. We must be competent team players. Deborah had herself together. She was clear about her purpose. Her authority was credible because it was audible. Do you know your purpose? We must have mutual respect. Each respected the other. He supported her request to enter battle; she agreed to respond to his need for her to accompany him.

Sisters, now that we understand men's role as brothers, let us go on to an even more daunting task—loving them.

## Reflection Questions

1. Why is a weakened woman a victim?
2. How do the writings of Paul regarding women and their lowered status affect you?
3. Have you ever held yourself back to allow a man to lead? Why?
4. Is it oppressive to restrict a woman from wearing pants in church?

# 8. Sins of the Father

"For nothing is hid that shall not be made manifest, nor anything secret that shall not be known and come to light." (Luke 8:17 NAS)

**We have tread** fearlessly and faithfully on our journey toward newness in Christ. We ardently are convinced that this millennium will not see us cowering in church corners. If we've come this far, we are daughters of New Faith. We have our faith, our Jesus, and our future. We are all somebody's daughters. A man somewhere biologically intersected a woman, and the rest is history. What does a daughter of New Faith look like? She isn't a blamer. She knows of her power to rise above tragedy. She is not a muzzled one; she is a truth teller. She is not passive; she is active. A daughter is more than a female child. Thus far we've turned the glaring light of womanist truth on our churches, our mothers, and ourselves. Now let's look at fatherhood and how it helps us and hurts us as daughters.

That's why this chapter delves into secrets—family secrets. Secrets have clutched the keys to our discomfort. Secrets have covered the reasons for our faltering. We bear the marks. We bear the stains. Black church women are well acquainted with the affects of fathers. Fathers or the lack of them have shaped not only our life outlook, but also our faith experience. Detrimental dads have an impact on women of faith, and their existence provides additional evidence as to why we have been religious victims. Underscoring their deeds is painful but necessary. New Faith gives voice to hurting women and applies balm to the wounds inflicted by sins of the father.

## We Must Turn on the Light

This is not a popular topic. Fathers of the faith, who hold fast to patriarchal tenets, do not like the light, but we must turn it on. For many daughters, their relationships with their fathers determine the way they see God and themselves as God's daughters. The word *father* summons forth a range of feelings in us—delight and depression, pain and pleasure.

For some sisters, daddy was a compassionate, loving, supportive role model. These women can sing the hymn, "This Is My Father's World" with the reassurance of an earthly daddy and a heavenly father. Yet for copious numbers of us, the word *father* rips our souls like a ragged razor. *Father* is the anger that rolls off momma's tongue right regularly. *Father* is the blank space on your birth certificate. *Father* is the roaming hands and erected penis at night. *Father* is a holiday visitor with a nervous smile, heavy cologne, and broken promises. He may be the father we yearned to know or the one we wish would go to hell, but his sins are ever before us. We've established in chapter 7 that God initially made men good. Their role of father is divinely designed. "Fathers have a parenting style that is significantly different from that of mothers, and the difference is important in healthy child development. According to the evidence, fathers make important contributions to their children's intellectual competence, prosocial and compassionate behavior, and psychological well-being."[1]

## Fathers in the Bible

God created fathers with so much power that they can harm their daughters by their presence or their absence. The harm can be intense, widespread, and long-lasting. In the biblical world, male children were preferred. Often daughters were considered a burden. The Scriptures offer scant images of fathers in positive relation to their daughters. We can only infer from the wording used and actions recorded that these particular men took interest in and time with their female children. One such positive relationship is found in Acts 21:9. It is the record of Philip, the father of virginal daughters who are all prophetesses. The fact that he is recorded in the Bible with them is exemplary, yet even more notable, Philip's daughters bear witness to the Acts 2:17b text ("and your daughters shall prophesy").

Another notable father is Jacob, who is presented as a father who cares about the welfare of his daughter Dinah. When Dinah is sexually assaulted by Shechem, Jacob responds by murdering Shechem and his entire clan in Genesis 34. With lenient eyes we read compassion and concern into the fatal acts that killed Shechem and his clan. We want to believe Jacob's motives were based on father-daughter love, not the patriarchal mindset that was enraged because his daughter (his property) was sullied.

Biblical fathers who are clearly victimizers of their daughters show us that sins of the father have been around awhile and that their daughters, in most instances, bear the stains of their sins. Lot and his two daughters are a lucid example of how fathers can damage their daughters' self-esteem. In Genesis 19:7 Lot's actions tell his daughters and the world that they are of little value and are highly expendable. He offers his two daughters as sexual fodder to the town's men, who had encircled his home demanding sexual intercourse with the male visitors inside. It is these same two daughters, devalued by their dad, who ultimately end up with father Lot in a cave after the destruction of Sodom and Gomorrah (Gen. 19:30). The women believe there are no other men for them in the world and make their father the father of their children. In Lot's drunken stupor he is led into sexual intercourse by his daughters. The cycle of depreciation continues.

In Genesis 30:23 Leah and Rachel are daughters of a deceitful father, Laban. Laban's deception infects his daughters with a lack of trust, compassion, and camaraderie for anyone. Laban tricks Jacob into marrying Leah after promising him Rachel. The father's tricks send the daughters into a mindless baby-producing frenzy to gain the love of a confused man. Their years of self-destructive behavior produce a passel of children and a legacy of doing foolish things to get a man.

David, the great king of Israel, is an emotionally absent father. He seemingly turns his back on his daughter Tamar after she is raped by her brother, his son Amnon. When David learns of the defilement of Tamar he is "very angry," yet he does nothing (2 Sam. 13:21). Another brother, Absolom, eventually avenges Tamar—some two years later. It is important to note that this story "never refers to David and Tamar as father and daughter! The father identifies with the son; the adulterer supports the rapist; male has joined male to deny justice to the female."[2] This father's estrangement from his daughter leaves her alone, afraid and lacking support. The Scriptures record that Tamar is thrown out of Amnon's presence like trash (2 Sam. 13:17). In her sorrow, "Tamar put ashes on her head, and rent the long robe which she wore; and she laid her hand on her head, and went away, crying aloud as she went" (2 Sam. 13:19).

The most gruesome father-daughter alliance is Jephthah and his daughter, found in Judges 11:29-40. Jephthah is known as a "mighty warrior" (11:1) who bargains with the elders for leadership of Gilead, should he win the battle against their warring enemies the Ammonites. Jephthah goes further and also strikes a bargain with God. He vows that if God grants him victory, "then whoever comes forth from the doors of my house to meet me, when I return victorious from the Ammonites, shall be the Lord's" (11:30). Upon his victory Jephthah's young, nameless daughter appears with tambourine and victory dance to meet her triumphant father. He tells her of the vow; she immediately acquiesces to her fate. Ultimately she is sacrificed. One biblical scholar has called the act "a faithless vow uttered by a foolish father."[3] This father "played" with God, and his daughter paid the price.

Daughters have looked to fathers for protection, support, and nurture, but they do not always find it. Generations of fathers who have not known how to appreciate daughters have created women with self-destructive tendencies. I suggest that the pews packed with girls minus their fathers are bound for the same centuries-old pitfalls as the biblical daughters—infighting, desperation to have men in their lives, and depression. This is why we flock to churches and stack our hopes on male preachers. They appear to be the ideal fathers. We hope and pray that they are. We bear the marks of all of them. New Faith identifies two arenas of trauma for daughters: fatherlessness and sexual abuse. The distress and discomfort must be tended to. To overcome this we must first face it.

## Fatherlessness

Black girls deserve fathers. When I was a girl, my dad meant the world to me. He was funny and friendly and consistently in my corner. He never wavered in encouraging me to strive. We have a lot in common. We are shameless night owls who can watch movies and eat fruit into the wee hours. We share a passion for writing. We also both stutter; I wish he'd kept that speech impediment to himself. I remember listening to the words stick in his throat like thorns and watching his mouth freezing in pronunciation position. It was as if the words were held prisoner. When the same happens to me, I see him, not me. Now that I am a woman, I can benefit from his love. I am fearless; I see no limitations. Girls without fathers aren't always so lucky.

A girl can grow up fatherless for a host of reasons. It is not her fault. It is never her fault; yet she will bear the brunt. Maybe her daddy died, or her parents were divorced, separated, or never married. Perhaps daddy was in prison, the military, or a remote job. Or her daddy could be in the home physically, but absent emotionally and socially. It is not her fault, but she bears the mark. New Faith asserts that growing up without a father is a sin because fathers' absence undermines the divine plan of God. His absence is a sin. His nonpresence cripples a part of us that should fly. We do not blame the daughters, but we shed light on the impact of fatherlessness to help women understand why they do what they do and help them make corrections and move onward toward more productive lives.

Fatherlessness is a widespread social plague. We cannot sing it or pray it away. It must be confronted. Statistics tell us that "40 percent of all girls in our society under the age of 18 will go to sleep in homes in which their fathers do not live."[4] And "the chances that by the age of 17 they will not be living with both biological parents stand at over 50 percent. Many studies have shown that the typical nonresident father neither supports nor even sees his children on a regular basis."[5]

We believe that the institution of fatherhood is deteriorating. This cannot be allowed to happen. Fathers are the first men in our lives, the one we need to be loved by first.

"A father plays a distinctive role in shaping a daughter's sexual style and her understanding of the male-female bond. A father's love and involvement builds a daughter's confidence in her own femininity and contributes to her sense that she is worth loving."[6]

We need our fathers. "A sense of love-worthiness gives young women a greater sense of autonomy and independence in later relationships with men. Consequently, women who have good relationships with their fathers are less likely to engage in an anxious quest for male approval or to seek male affection through promiscuous sexual behavior."[7] Even worse, when fatherless women "are deprived of a stable relationship with a nonexploitative adult male who loves them, these girls can remain developmentally "stuck" struggling with issues of security and trust that well-fathered girls have already successfully resolved."[8]

## We Are Stuck

*Stuck* is an appropriate word for us. We are stuck in ways of being with no understanding of how we got here. We are in the pews imploding left and right and clueless as to why. These behaviors surface in church as well as the community, and they impede God's plan for us. Absent fathers create women who are angry and do not know why they are angry. Angry church women are known for their legendary "attitudes." They are known as "not the ones to mess with." Often these sisters are admired by the congregation, when all the while they need to be rescued from their anger. Such sisters have carefully crafted a reputation around the church as the ones who set people straight and figure them out at the drop of a dime.

"I don't play," said Sister Mangrove dryly and curtly. "Playtime is out. I get to the point." This woman's scowl was renowned. At the age of seventy-five, Sister Mangrove had spent her lifetime being curt and pointed. She could and would scare many a sinner straight. But being mad all the time was not God's plan for her.

Absent fathers create women who perpetually degrade themselves even though they are more than able. As a pastor, I am saddened that often women are reluctant to step forward to serve and even lead in church government. It is often an arm-twisting experience to get some women who are qualified to lead. "I can't serve on the committee: I'm not smart enough; I'm not educated enough," they whine. The reverse is true with men: Whether they are qualified or not, they eagerly take on leadership.

In many churches fatherless women are waiting to experience love from a God in the form of a man known as father. The difficulty arises because the women don't know how a father should properly love them. This void of knowledge leaves them open, vulnerable, and disconnected from the truth. We don't know how to be fathers' daughters.

"Yes, I know the feeling," said Mari, who grew up with her two siblings in a single-parent home. "Mom did the best she could. She worked all types of jobs to make it. But I still know the feeling of not having a father. My dad died when I was five years old. A part of me will never feel whole. Often I wonder what activities my dad and I would have done together if he had lived. I fantasize about how my dad would look now as an older man. I look at a gray-haired man who might be my father's age when I walk down the street and I pretend it is him. Church has always been a comforting place for me. God stepped in and became my daddy."

Noted authors such as Alice Walker and Bebe Campbell Moore have penned books about fatherlessness. Author Sheneska Jackson writes also on this topic in her novel *Lil Momma's Rules*. Jackson's main character "Madison McQuire" illustrates that fatherlessness can sand down rough corners on our personalities. Her jagged portrait of "missing-in-action" daddy shoves rage in our faces. "I was telling the truth. My daddy was a low-down, mangy, flea-infested dog. He got my mother pregnant with me and after I was born he wouldn't even claim me. Said he didn't know if I was really his or not. Said he wanted to take a blood test, but he never did. It wasn't necessary after I turned four years old and became his spitting image. This overbite I got—his. After a while it was too obvious who my daddy was but even after all that, he really never claimed me. Never moved in to help my mother and help raise me."[9]

What this specifically means for church women is that we must look at our wounds. We must assess the damage and resist further infection. The father void makes us all the more compliant to the leadership of men, less likely to be leaders ourselves, and less likely to support other women in leadership. We long to be a daughter to the father—any man in authority. We are eager for a command, an order, and a chance to be somebody's daughter. We hunger for a man to submit to. We want to please the father figure in our lives and experience the anticipated inner warmth and satisfaction of accomplishment. We are prime targets for abuse in church.

I'll never forget this scene: The women of this church functioned like children, and the pastor functioned like their daddy. At the sound of his footsteps, the women scurried around the sanctuary like excited children. They knew what he required—water at room temperature, handkerchief placed exactly to the right of the Bible—and were ready to meet those requirements. He was their pastor, father, guardian, and more. They were daughters of the church. Whatever he said was the law. His needs were met. His ways were the gospel. This was his world. This warm, cozy place fulfilled all of their needs—the pastor's need to control and the women's need to be controlled.

The absence of fathers sows seeds of long-term destruction. According to a "national survey of women aged fifteen to forty-four, women who spend part of their childhoods in one-parent families are more likely to marry and bear children early, to give birth before marriage, and to have their own marriages break up."[10] These statistics foretell a future of threefold catastrophe: unprepared women who rush into marriage and family commitments, the bearing of children outside of marriage, and dissolution of marriages. Each of these three is destructive enough to live on for generations of women if we do not work for change now. New Faith says, in the name of Jesus, no more.

As daughters of New Faith, fatherless women are encouraged to learn themselves and determine if they are angry, weak, or overly passive with men. This assessment can come from a book you read, a class you enroll in, or sage advice from an elder. It should be noted, however, that the importance of fathers does not condemn mothers who are doing an awesome job all by themselves. We seek to continuously encourage men who are fathers to be who God has called them to be—responsible. It should also be noted that while fathers are necessary, when they are abusive to their wives and children, they become unnecessary. Violence is never acceptable in a relationship. Moreover, fatherless families should know that they can succeed and function as a healthy family unit; single mothers and their children survive and, yes, thrive alone.

We have a role to play in reversing the demise of Dad. Good fathers must be encouraged and treasured. We can salvage the troubled fathers with prayer. Our churches can encourage men to organize dads' clubs, fathering classes, and support groups. We can prepare our boys to be future dads by rearing them with strong commitment to family. We also rear them with discipline and determination to rid ourselves of the old expectation of "raising our daughters and loving our sons." We must make a better world for our daughters by deglamorizing single-mothering-by-choice and cohabitation. Both leave children unprotected. Even though enormously famous recording artists assume this role easily and effortlessly, it is nevertheless detrimental to children and contrary to the will of God. Fathers are necessary and not "just for their sperm."[11] Today's women do not necessarily need fathers for provision. They have jobs, degrees, and bank accounts. Today's women do not need fathers for protection. They have self-defense classes, 911, and Smith and Wesson. Fathers are necessary because they are from God.

## Sexual Abuse

As difficult as it is to believe, growing up with a spiritually corrupt father in the home can be more dangerous than growing up without a father at all. Incest is quietly rampant. I knew the dictionary meaning of *incest,* but I did not accept the word as real until I was a sophomore in college. "Allie," a childhood friend of my college roommate, breezed through my life on her way to Paris to meet a much older boyfriend on her spring break. She spent one day in our dormitory room with us and changed my life forever. Her mannerisms enchanted me. I'd never met a woman my age so mature and worldly. Her talk of older men, clothes, and travel dazzled me. "I have a trail of men across the world," she said with a sly smile, "and I hate them all."

She inadvertently left behind a bottle of her expensive perfume on the dresser. I remarked to my roommate, "Wow. This is the kind of perfume she wears?" She replied nonchalantly, "You need to know her father buys her all that stuff—the perfume, clothes, airline tickets—to cover up. He's been having sex with her since elementary school." I gasped at the revelation. That moment was the first time incest had ever entered my thoughts or my mind. I asked myself, "Allie and her father? Why didn't somebody help her back then? Is it too late? Do fathers intentionally maim their daughters?"

"Allie was not the only one," I reasoned. "There were probably others. Maybe some on my block back home or in my Sunday school." I felt like the world had known a secret and had not let me in on it. This revelation jabbed my soul like an ice pick. I hurt for Allie and all the other girls I had known but had not known the truth about.

The national statistics showed me how correct I was. "Estimates suggest that at least one in three women is a victim of childhood sexual abuse."[12] Additional research tells us that ". . . a daughter is molested by her father every thirty minutes."[13] "Sexual abuse of children is not about sex or love. It is about the abuse of power, control and authority."[14] Some women don't even realize they were molested during their childhood. The behavior may have been "normal" in their homes. Or it could have been the little secret kept by threats.

Sexual abuse comes in many forms.

> It can be sexual touching while bathing or diapering a child. It can be masturbating in front of the child or coaxing or forcing her to watch adults have sex. Abuse could be taking nude photographs of the child or talking about sex in order to derive pleasure. Abuse can be cloaked in "accidents" such as opening the door to the bathroom or bedroom when the child is undressed or inappropriate staring. Abuse can be shrouded by concern such as unnecessary, intrusive medical interventions such as enemas or vaginal exams.[15]

Sexual abuse in Christian homes from Scripture-quoting daddies is not rare. The Christian home has been a hiding place for daddy's sexual sins. Girls who grow up in these confusing circumstances question how the God they loved could allow this awful act to take place. One sister-preacher told her story in *Essence*. "I am the daughter of a Black pastor who raped me from the time that I was eleven years old. And my mother acted as though this didn't happen. And my daddy told me, 'If you tell your momma, it will probably kill her; she's already had one heart attack.' Then he cited the story of Lot's daughters in Scripture and said, 'This is of God.'"[16]

Kayla is another woman living with a childhood of incest. Her father molested her for many years of her childhood. Her dad was and still is a deacon and Sunday-school teacher at their church. He would fondle her breasts and vagina when her mother was away. Kayla was too stunned to cry out for help. Over time a pattern developed. The abuse occurred when mother would leave for midweek prayer service at church. The father and daughter would always come to church later. Kayla said, "I was too confused about the emotions I felt. I love him and I hate him. My dad was the pride of the family and the church. Deacon Brown could be depended on to take care of the sick, pray for the bereaved and pay any member's overdue bills. He was loved by all," she said. Today Kayla is thirty-seven, still confused, and still living at home with her parents. This is not rare. "The idea of saying no to the emotional demands of a parent, spouse or authority figure may be practically inconceivable. Thus it is not uncommon to find adult survivors who continue to minister to the wishes and needs of those who once abused them."[17]

We must also include a daughter's potential danger of sexual abuse from any male—mother's boyfriends, family friends, brothers, uncles, cousins, and more. Simply put, female children are targets. Once the innocence has been taken, the girl needs a power greater than herself to restore her original love for herself. In street lingo, this abuse messes with your head. High-profile sisters such as Maya Angelou, Oprah Winfrey, and Iyanla Van Zant have exposed their wounds of girlhood incest to the fresh air of truth. Maybe if more of us talked, told the truth, and gave the names of our perpetrators, violating men would be hunted down and imprisoned.

According to therapists, "childhood abuse appears to have a significant relationship with these women's later ability to trust God's love and care, as well as the ability to put their painful experiences into some meaningful framework."[18] Victims have "fundamental problems in basic trust, autonomy, and initiative. They approach the task of early adulthood—establishing independence and intimacy—burdened by major impairments in self-care and the capacity to form stable relationships."[19]

One writer says, "the sexualization of children is not separable from the issue of power and control, and the equation of male sexuality with aggression and dominance."[20] This means that the victimization of girls is tied to the male need to control. When these hurting, harmed sisters come to church, their woundedness is in even greater danger of continuation and intensification. The patriarchal disposition of the African American church makes it a potentially lethal place. Thus, women who have been wounded by patriarchally based incest may then face patriarchally based sexism. Our churches want to keep on having church in this grim darkness without acknowledging the dimness. Few have dared turn on the light.

## Survivors, Not Victims

The behavior of abused women in the church becomes problematic for a number of reasons. One in particular is the abused woman's potential relationship with her pastor. "In a quest for rescue, she may seek out powerful authority figures who seem to offer the promise of special care taking relationships."[21] If not the pastor, then other men may fill that role. "Inevitably, however, the chosen person may fail to live up to her fantastic expectations.

When disappointed, she may furiously denigrate the same person whom she so recently adored. Ordinary interpersonal conflicts may provoke intense anxiety, depression, and rage. In the mind of the survivor, even minor slights evoke past experiences of callous neglect, and minor hurts evoke past experiences of deliberate cruelty. Thus the survivor develops a pattern of intense, unstable relationships, repeatedly enacting dramas of rescue, injustice and betrayal."[22]

The abuse we've endured has had a negative impact on our faith. We are emotionally and sometimes spiritually arrested and easy prey for the sexism of the church. I wondered why we did not fight back; now I know. There is a way out. "When one feels ashamed, worthless, discounted and devalued, strategies are needed to recover a sense of worth and value."[23] Some researchers have found that "schooling, career, and finding a meaningful life task were important factors for sexually abused women."[24]

New Faith urges women to be survivors and not victims of their pasts. As with fatherless women, women with sexual-abuse histories can and should expect the church to help, not to prolong their pain. New Faith insists that churches break the cycle of painful lives. Perpetrators must be revealed and punished. Sermons should regularly talk about sins of the fathers. The journey toward recovery begins here. We insist that an abused woman can no longer live with her wounds in hiding. The bright sunshine of reality is her healing point. Persecution and domination serve only to deepen the wound.

New Faith believes that forgiveness does not mean acquiescing to abuse, letting the victimizer escape punishment, or pretending it did not happen. Forgiveness is freeing yourself from the pain so you can move on. Dr. Linda Hollies states even more plainly in her book, *Taking Back My Yesterdays*, that forgiveness is essential. "I was sitting, reflecting on my own life, feeling down and wanting to have a pity party, and the tears began to flow freely. But they were not for me, the poor victim. These tears were for him, the poor victimizer. I cried for the loss of his childhood. His mother died and his father 'got lost' before he was seven years old. He didn't get to develop that necessary sense of security. His world was not a safe place where for just a little while he was the center of their universe. I cried for him. He needed my tears."[25]

Jesus tell us in Luke 8:17 that the truth will come forth. The light is healing. Our fathers have hurt and harmed us, but we must choose to reveal their sins and press on. Get therapy if need be, but press on. We are collectively turning on the lights so the world will see how competent, strong, and beautiful we are.

## Reflection Questions

1. What emotions does the word *father* provoke in you?
2. What kind of impact do you think the biblical fathers have on father-daughter relationships?
3. Should the church have a role in the healing process of incest victims and victimizers?

# 9. It's Time for Love

"O Daughters of Jerusalem, I adjure you, do not stir up love before it is time." (Song of Solomon 8:4 NAS)

**Loving a man** has been a precipitous practice of ours from the beginning of time. Loving a man will destroy us if we don't know ourselves, or if we don't believe that we are wonderfully and fearfully made, or if our souls are still on the plantation. The truth is, we women have been damaged in the throes of courtship, dating, or even just a simple lunch. It's not that men are bad; they are not. We've affirmed their worth in chapter 5. The way we've been taught to love them has been hazardous to our health. Yet in the face of historical peril, New Faith declares it is time to stir up love.

## Sisters Awake and Aware

New Faith is adamant that loving a man is optional—not required. You can still have joy in Jesus whether you have a man or not. Single women and New Faith combine to configure a redemptive woman who enjoys who she is because she knows who she is. She enjoys the company of men, but she does not have the "hungry-eyed dog" look about her. She is somebody with or without. It is her choice. And if you choose, it's time for love.

I speak of heterosexual love because my life experiences have been heterosexual. I possess no personal knowledge of homosexuality, and I feel I cannot appropriately tell a story belonging to gay and lesbian people. The absence of lesbian voices and experiences from these pages does not seek to deny their presence in the Black community.

My sisters, let's tarry by the waters of love to reflect on how far we've come in New Faith. We can pause for a moment in this hard-fought, demanding, grueling pilgrimage. You have been brave, strong, and hearty of spirit to arrive at this point. Your very presence at this milestone is your entitlement to love. The strongest of us love the best. Heightened self-awareness and strengthened boundaries have been developed along your way. It is time for love because we are at a place of internal peace. Bell hooks was right when she said, "We cannot make love on a battlefield."[1] New Faith gives us the authority to turn the battlefield of yesterday into the blessing of today. Our men are worth loving and loving assiduously. It's time for love. If you desire it, the love of a man should be yours.

New Faith declares that love is not a game for fools. We are not in the mood for games. New Faith will not permit you to be a foolish woman in love. "Why do fools fall in love?" the popular recording asks. First of all, fools assume that being in love means a downward spiral. Male-female love should be an upward ascension. If we fall down into love, we can be hurt. If we intentionally step up and into love, we are aware of our actions and where we are going. Isn't it time for us to know where we are going in our relationships with men?

Many of us have been ignorant about relationships and accepting of anything that comes our way. "Thank you, Jesus, I've got a man—or at least a piece of one" is the motto of droves of single sisters who pack the pews like sitting ducks waiting for a man to smile their way. The word is out that single women in the church are naive, easily conned, and desperate. No more.

Meet Monica. She's prayed, fasted, and thought through the decision to have a man in her life. Her conclusion: "Yes, I want one. But he will arrive my way or not at all." New Faith brings new expectations and approaches to relationships. Things don't just happen anymore. We are awake and aware. Silence was golden back in the day. Our foremothers were seen and not heard. We must love differently now. New Faith defines love as a whole self who chooses to be engaged with another whole self for mutual connection that follows Jesus. This love is not platonic or demonstrated on the sly; it must be real and seen in the light of day. Love means caring about him, but not at the expense of self.

It is not just sex; it is not him paying your rent or taking you on a cruise. Love is respect; it is the tone of voice. It is commitment, follow-through, unconditional devotion. It is equality in everything. Surely by now it is clear that unnecessary suffering is a relic of the twentieth century. All else is perfumed bondage. Bondage is where we have languished and labored in a confused, desperate daze. No more. In the patriarchy called our lifetimes, love has been another form of enslavement. Loving a man meant voluntarily stepping into a vise grip of unyielding gender roles and regulation. Loving a man meant chasing a man—but not appearing to—and falling prey to every double standard ever written. Men phone women; women don't phone men. Men ask women out on dates; women do not ask a man out on dates. Loving a man meant giving up something that God told you to hold on to—such as your self-respect, dignity, and self-esteem—because the man was too fine for you to let him go. Many a backseat sex session was aimed at securing the fidelity of Mr. Fine himself. Where was God in all of this chaos that was mislabeled as love?

## Putting Slavery behind Us

New Faith believes that God was there all the while, waiting for us to come back to our strong, wise, noble selves. We were not designed to be played on or over in relationships. It is not God's plan that we carry baggage and scars from one relationship to the next, unable to find peace.

Norman was the first boy that I vividly remember loving. Love was a safe exhilaration. We were fifth graders at Oaklawn Elementary School, and love for us—well really, me—was letting other kids know that I loved him. I hoped that he'd let the same kids know that he felt the same. Love for me meant being demonstrative. So I scribbled Norman's name all over my Converse sneakers. This upset my father to no end. He reasoned, "Norman did not purchase the shoes, so how does he rate having his name all over them?" Love for me was the elation of the heart, the expectation of the spirit, and the thrill of anticipation. I was free to be me, and he was free to be who he was. Black women and God have strayed away from this privilege and stumbled into a repetitive begging syndrome. We take what we can get and pray God will make him better. As a pastor who routinely counsels single women on the men issue, the begging and the settling habits trouble me most. Why do we beg and settle? It is a form of sacrificing. How did the sacrificing begin?

During slavery equality existed between men and women. Kelly Brown Douglas notes that during slavery, "Enslaved men and women related to each other as equals. They engaged in complementary and reciprocal relationships. Any other kinds of relationships would have proven disastrous for the well-being of their sons and daughters, as well as for themselves."[2] After slavery, the real battle commenced. Freedom must have been a frightening condition for our men. Once the chains were removed from their wrists and ankles, they made it their first order of business to place the chains back on their women. A rigid type of thinking invaded Black love after slavery. Records indicate that slave women were often skilled leaders who were

> captains of the industry in the fields, with supervision of men. Apparently the freedmen did not want to perpetuate a model of authority subordinating black men to black women. In the Reconstruction era, Negro males, like white males, asserted themselves by insisting that wives spend more time in home management and less in field work, by demanding that mothers care for their children, and by exhibiting such common masculine exclusiveness as leaving the wives at home while they themselves attended fraternal and political gatherings. In legal and economic matters, black men assumed the power to speak for their wives and children.[3]

Freedom for them did not mean freedom for us. The church mirrored the suppression of women. Specific research culled from written records of Black Methodist preachers' meetings of the Washington Annual Conference between 1872 and 1890 indicates precisely where women stood. The question was asked "Is woman inferior to man?" "The chairman of the meeting stated, 'Sad as it may be, woman is as inferior to man as man is to God.'"[4] It can be accurately deduced that the church believed us inferior and that the relationships between men and women mirrored our perceived inferior status. Thus the church and church men understood their duty to keep God's order. Love—their way—kept us in line. Relationships were designed as the first step of our faith-based surrender.

## Love Our Way

New Faith says it's time for love our way. I offer the love lyrics of Song of Solomon as our spiritual backdrop.

Why? They are bold, independent, and educating. I do this to rouse our appetite for robust love. We must be liberated from the dungeons of anger, depression, and frustration. We deserve to feel the lushness of love that has been long denied. Song of Solomon is the language of a Black woman head over heels in love. Yes, she is black. In chapter 1 she states, "I am black and beautiful" (1:5 NRSV). We need to hear a female voice teach us about love. She is speculated to be the Queen of Sheba: maybe so, maybe not. She is a ". . . savvy teacher who passes her knowledge on to her impressionable female admirers. Love has taught her a few things about herself, about the opposite sex, about stolen intimacy, about love itself. She has learned that love must be allowed to run its course, neither interfered with nor prematurely provoked."[5]

The power of the patriarchy prevented the Song of Solomon from being called, "When a woman loves a man." But it is all right. This sister's eloquent journey into love is not necessarily a perfect one. But whose is? She states in Song of Solomon 5:10: "My beloved is dazzling and ruddy outstanding among ten thousand . . . his mouth is full of sweetness. And he is wholly desirable. This is my beloved and this is my friend, O daughter of Jerusalem." She is doing what New Faith requires of us: Don't hesitate, step out, and move toward the goal. If you fall, girl, get up, learn your lesson, and keep moving. Teach others about your steps, and help them on their pathway. We heed her warning. Love can be dangerous, damaging, and damning. We have the benefit of centuries of progress. We will be brave, smart, and proactive in love—this time.

It's time for love. We of the twenty-first century say it's time. The woman in Song of Solomon did not have the access to power that we do. Sometimes it's hard to admit that we want to be loved. To do so would confess a vulnerability and neediness. The mantra of the 1990s was "I don't need a man." Single women proclaimed their ability to go it alone. They could and still can. The issue is that love is one of those luxuries long denied African American women. People expect us to be strong and fearless. People expect us to maintain a boisterous love for Jesus and for everyone else in the world. But what about us? We've been so much for so many for so long. We've been expected to love everybody and forget about our needs. "Many black females have learned to deny our inner needs while we develop our capacity to cope and confront in public life. This is why we can often appear to be functioning well on jobs, but be utterly dysfunctional in private."[6] You know the sister (or you are she) who seems in charge of her professional life but is in disarray socially, especially with men.

Mia was a medical student who was also active in her church. She was obviously scholastically tight. Her academic successes propelled her through the rigors of medical school and into a specialized program. She was easy to admire—a Black woman doing well in a high-pressure, highly intellectualized world where we are usually rare and unwelcome. And all the while she soared medically, she failed with men. "I'd go for the wrong ones every time," she said. "My last boyfriend was a closet crack addict; before him I was dating a guy who borrowed my credit card and ran up a $5,000 bill; and the one before him was married. Why am I so unlucky?" she said. "I want someone, but I don't want to be hurt."

Mia and many other women need New Faith in their lives, lest they be destroyed by their search for love. New Faith would not deter Mia from being intimate with men but would give her a foundation to understand herself, set her standards, and stand on them. Let's admit our need to be loved and our lack of skills in the love department. Churches owe us lessons on love. Somewhere between vacation church school and Bible study, we missed something. Yet we were expected to grow from girls and into church women who knew how to love. Or was the intent to leave us groping in the dark? Yes, we are overdue for instruction. New Faith offers six belated love lessons. Please accept them with interest.

1. *All of us must have boundaries.* Boundaries are the lines of demarcation that separate us from other people in healthy ways. They give us our individuality and help us maintain and monitor our sense of safety and well-being. Look at the space immediately around your body—the front, back, and both sides. Place a border there. That is your space, and what others do while in your space is your decision alone. Our boundaries are the foundation of our self-esteem and self-love.

2. *You can love him without losing yourself.* For some sisters, finding a man to love is the excuse they need to misplace themselves. It is easy to bury their hopes, dreams, and aspirations in him as though he were some type of savior. This seems to be a female birth defect. We sacrifice self and lower self in order to have him. It is called "de-selfing." It means that "too much of one's self (including one's thoughts, wants, beliefs, and ambition) is negotiable under pressures from the relationship."[7]

3. *You should lose the romance.* Romance should be packed away with the other relics of the twentieth century. It is a trap. Romance is like high heels in a marathon race: It gets in the way, slows you down, and is out of place. Romance has messed up many a sister. I am not dismissing the passion and ardor that arises between a man and a woman. I am dismissing our tendency to blow out of proportion such occasions. Romance is the fatal fantasy that lures us into relationships with men that we should be running from. Romance is an anesthetic used to deaden and numb the sensation of truth. Flowers can overwhelm us; candy and jewels can blind us to what is really going on. A blind woman in love is a woman headed for trouble. Trade it in on reality. Some say that romance is the

bait, and we are the fish being caught. "Romance was necessary not only to give form to male adventures and female lives but also to maintain marriage itself. For if marriage is seen without its romantic aspects, it ceases to be attractive to its female half and hence, is no longer useful to its patriarchal supporters."[8]

4. *You should cut your losses* rather than going down with the relationship and/or the man. When it's over, it's over. Sometimes prayer and fasting gets you the same answer that God was probably saying from the start: It's over. The years of your continual tears, yelling, or cussing him won't change him. You must learn to let it go if it's not working. The new millennium won't allow us to bring in needless baggage. "Black women have tried for years to save the lives of black men. We have stayed in destructive relationships trying to hold it all together. And one of the most meaningful lessons self-recovery teaches us is that it is the individual's acceptance of responsibility for changing, for 'saving' his or her own life."[9]

5. *Sexual abstinence for single women remains a foundation,* because it serves God and us well. Abstinence is not designed to make life drab. Sex outside marriage is an arena where traditionally women get shortchanged. We live in what's called a "phallocracy." This is a place where the phallus, or penis, rules. Most things are controlled by, fueled by, or done to impress, engage, or arouse the phallus. If the phallus rules the world, sex is a game we cannot win. The sexual revolution of the 1970s and 1980s led us to believe that if we were single and sexually active, we gained power. The only gain was children out of wedlock and being forced to raise them on our own. Our "freedom" gave men the license to be absent. That's why New Faith advocates celibacy. In other words, we don't have to have it! We can find fulfillment in other areas of life.

"I have been celibate for four years," Tonya told the group of women. "I went from 'she's gotta have it,' to 'I can do without it.' I know all about sex, and I know how fornication displeases God. For a long time, I did not care what God thought. It was about my needs and me. Years ago I found myself sexually addicted to a man who cared nothing for me. I decided that I could do bad all by myself. Just like that, I stopped. I wanted to see if I could live without it, and I can."

6. *Money can be a pitfall.* Smart sisters understand that money in their hands is power. Money spent by a woman on a date gives her leverage and lessens her chances of being the victim. Resisting the temptation to be taken care of gives us the equal footing we need to ensure that the relationship remains on the track we have in mind. New Faith recommends equal paying for dates. Regina can testify to this. "I realized after twenty years of dating that as soon as I sat back and let him pay, I lost control. He felt like he owned me. Never again. The more they spend on you, the more they want in return," she said.

## Dating

We deserve to be loved. Sisters, it's time to stir up love—with control, even precision and premeditation. Single sisters, dating is one of the most powerful acts we have at our disposal. In the dating arena, we choose, we decide, we select. It is the privilege of power that we seize. New Faith goes to the Bible for a scriptural basis for dating. There we continue to find women boldly being who God called them to be. There was a biblical woman who was assertive in this area. Her name was Ruth. She decided it was time for love, and she went after the man she wanted. Ruth's mother-in-law, Naomi, choreographed the assertive dating steps. Ruth wanted a relationship, and with guts, good timing, and faith, she succeeded. You know the story. Let's see it afresh through the eyes of New Faith.

In chapter one of the book of Ruth, we meet Ruth and Naomi, who are both widows. Ruth decides to remain with her mother-in-law even though her sister-in-law, Orpah, returns home to her original home. The two widows journey from Moab to Bethlehem in order to find food. While in Bethlehem, Ruth, with the benefit of Naomi's coaching, identifies the man she wants (Boaz) and places herself near him. She approaches, acts, and achieves. Naomi reasons to her daughter-in-law, "My daughter, should I not seek a home for you, that it may be well with you? Now is not Boaz our kinsman, with whose maidens you were? See, he is winnowing barley tonight at the threshing floor. Wash therefore and anoint yourself, and put on your best clothes and go down to the threshing floor" (3:1-3). The story ends with Ruth securing her man.

Dating is a powerful act that we must master. Never underestimate what you and God can accomplish. Dating is the way I learned myself. I learned to establish boundaries. It defined my personhood. I've dated my share of trifling, confused, and immature men. They were outnumbered by plenty of charming, suave, and gregarious men. I am better for both types of men. When dates did not work out well, I learned that I was not a failure; the date was. Also I learned what type of man I was not successful with. All men were not my type, and the process of trial and error benefited me. My understanding of self increased with every date, as did my confidence in myself to learn what was good and what was bad for me.

One summer night, while in post-baccalaureate study at Howard University, I met a very cute guy named Jacques. Early in the initial conversation it was clear that he was not my type. But I gave him my phone number anyway. A few days later when Jacques invited me to a crab boil, he was just getting a sympathy date. I did not like him, but I wanted something to do that night. He probably felt the same way, too. He did not even bother to open the door of the car when we reached his mother's house. I didn't open it either. He left me sitting in the car. I sat there because I did not care about him or the date. We were both stubborn. The date was spent apart. He was inside enjoying a crab dinner with his family while I sat outside in the car. It was a valuable lesson: Don't date guys you don't even like.

There was the time I learned the importance of staying out of guy's apartments. Clearly, if a woman does not want to have sex with a guy, she should avoid visits to his abode. Clayton invited me over for dinner and a movie. I was quite naive and was clueless that I would be the dessert. After prying his hands off my body for the third time, I headed for the door, only to catch a barrage of insults hurled at my exit. "You tease. Why did you even come over here?" he screamed. The Lord allowed me to escape so that I might testify. Date in safe, open, well-lit places.

In the past, dating was not considered our choice. The traditional interpretation of Proverbs 18:22 ("He who finds a wife finds a good thing") has kept us sitting in the house or dreaming of the day when he will speak to us because we dare not speak to him. It has kept us in relationship handcuffs, waiting and anticipating a phone call or an invitation. We wondered if he would even look at us or strike up a conversation. This one biblical passage cannot dictate the entire dating design.

If you see or meet a man to whom you are attracted, you can speak to him. You can even begin a conversation with him. Invite him out to dinner, to church, or to the movies. You need not wait to be plucked or chosen like a car sitting on a car lot. New Faith gives you a framework for selecting a man who is eligible for you. Develop a profile, a checklist. Yes, faith and prayer are prominent, but so is common sense. You must know yourself, your strengths, your weaknesses, your assets, and your liabilities. You can choose men who complement—rather than compromise—you. New Faith women are certain, not waffling on choices about men.

## The Men We Want

We want men who are clean inside and out. A deliberate walk with Christ is cleansing. Psalm 51:10 tells us: "Create in me a clean heart, O God." One of the most common dirty spots is pornography. This filth taints the soul. Many men consider porn harmless, but nothing could be further from the truth. Once God has cleaned up the inside, the outside should naturally follow. We like men with clean clothes, faces, teeth, and hands, too.

We want men who are able to work consistently. The ability to get a job and keep a job is vital. Sadly, some brothers have developed a taste for the "bread of idleness" described in Proverbs 31:27. We are not demanding that all men earn a six-figure income, drive an expensive car, or work in a skyscraper. We simply want a man who gets up and goes to work someplace every day. We want men who are compassionate. We want them to put on a "heart of compassion," as described in Colossians 3:12. Too often brothers get stuck in the tough-guy, man-of-steel motif. They stuff their emotions way down inside and disconnect with us. An emotionally distant man is crippled in many ways.

We want men who are big enough to confess or admit when they are wrong. Few things are worse than being around someone who is never wrong. It takes guts to say, "Baby, I was wrong," and that's exactly what we want to hear when he is in error. It is also biblical. In James 5:16 we learn, "Confess your sins to one another." We want men who understand the need to communicate with common sense. No one enjoys being talked to recklessly or wickedly. There is a right way and a wrong way to disagree, make a point, and share an opinion. In Proverbs 13:3 we learn, "He who guards his mouth preserves his life."

We want men who are credible instead of creeps. Credible men are those who do what they say and say what they do, particularly in the area of relationships. The lies and games of creeps have ruined many women. These scoundrels have biblical roots. In 2 Tim. 3:6 we learn, "For among them are those who make their way into households and capture weak women." We want men who during their single days are sexually celibate. In some instances the Christianity of a man comes to a screeching halt in the area of sex. They say: That's the one area where surely the Lord didn't mean it. Sisters sometimes find themselves in wrestling matches trying to preserve their bodies for marriage. In 1 Corinthians 7:1 we learn, "It is well for a man not to touch a woman."

Loving a man is taking a gamble. New Faith prepares us for this risk. If you choose to pause by the waters of love, be armed with prayer, common sense, self-love, and bravery. Stir up love. Pursue love. You have earned the privilege of knowing what you want and going after it. Let us press on. There are deeper waters to cross.

## Reflection Questions

1. Are single sisters easily conned by men?
2. Does loving a man mean giving up or losing something?
3. How does Song of Solomon give us voice?
4. Should you be as aggressive with men as Ruth was?

# 10 Becoming One Flesh

"... and they shall become one flesh." (Gen. 2:24)

**W**hen **New Faith** combines with marriage, it creates a union that makes God smile. (All of her teeth are showing this time.) New Faith finally gives women and men what they deserve from marriage—authentic intimacy. We have been at each other's throats long enough. Intimacy is the answer. Intimacy cannot exist where husbands are dominating bosses or wives are submissive serfs. Husbands and wives are partners in a sacred trust ordained by God. This partnership creates one flesh from two lives.

## New Faith Partnering

Working with our men instead of against them, we can achieve what was unthinkable in the past century. Intimacy means no more games, pretense, or superficial interactions. Intimacy means we can be who we are in a relationship and allow the other person to do the same. "An intimate relationship is one in which neither party silences, sacrifices, or betrays the self and each party expresses strength and vulnerability, weakness and competence in a balanced way."[1]

New Faith asserts that when the first man and woman became "one flesh," it was God's design to birth an intimacy—a marriage, not a hierarchical flowchart. Adam and Eve brought their strengths and weaknesses to the coupling, and they shared them. They were not squabbling over who cooked or who mowed the lawn. They realized fairly quickly that they needed each other in order to survive. Their interdependence was more important than who called the shots.

Life after the Garden of Eden has not been kind to marriage. This institution has rapidly deteriorated and become a trick bag for women. Historically, women sought marriage for protection but withered under its harsh taskmaster known as "women's work." Take away marriage's romance and myths and all that's left is the raw truth: Marriage has been the institutionalizing of "men's exchange of women's sexual, reproductive, childbearing, and other domestic services for material or political gains."[2] Sisters, we are too precious in the sight of the Lord to marry into misery. Unnecessary suffering is not a part of marriage. New Faith is convinced that the same Jesus, who brought us thus far, does not want to see women paired off and tethered to draining utility connections with no voice, no power, and no vote.

The chapters of this book have sketched a continual string of evidence from our Africa to our present to prove that the patriarchal Black church crippled us. Marriage is no different. It promises one thing and delivers another. The type of marriages we were encouraged to subscribe to were beautifully decorated snares. Love à la church is a land blanketed with our bruised and broken bodies. Our limbs are snared in the paradox of loving him but silencing ourselves. The church taught us to give up our power religiously, socially, and culturally for love. Black women, like all women, have historically given away their lives, passions, interests, and power in the name of love, commitment, and marriage. Women who should have been doctors, lawyers, and preachers stepped down from their aspirations to marry.

I've known women like that. They were smart, talented, and ambitious young women who were college class-mates of mine. They enrolled in challenging degree pro-grams like engineering, biochemistry, and law. Yet all the while their goals were not the academic Bachelor of Arts or Bachelor of Science degrees. They sought the highly favored "MRS" degree. Their parents sent them to college to marry and to marry well. Anything less was failure. That's a tremendous price to pay for a band of gold and a lifetime of housework. It should never be one or the other. We want both—marriage and a life.

## Costs of Traditional Marriage

Love in the patriarchy is not a threat to women who do not think. Non-thinking women cheerfully descend into the role of second-class citizen, and from the courtship to the wedding, they enjoy the ride. Conservative Christian groups such as the Promise Keepers and Focus on the Family made the late 1990s prime time for male domination in the home. They defined godly relationships from the male perspective. If men were in charge, the relationship was godly. Errant men were urged to go home and be the providers, the pro-tectors, and involved in their children's lives.

What's wrong with that? Nothing. The problem is that these groups urged men to function as the leader with complete control and responsibility for all decisions, thoughts, ideas, and dreams. Thus, the husband's return is the wife's signal to sit down and shut up. The intelligent, shrewd, and decisive management the wife executed while he was gone is now null and void. In this scenario, men rule, women take orders, and God is pleased.

A number of the high-profile African American pastors with television ministries also preach this sexist message.

Using Ephesians 5:22, "Wives, be subject to your husbands, as to the Lord," they proclaim that God will not bless a home where the man does not lead. Week in and week out thousands of sisters, who continue to dominate such churches, stand to their feet, and bellow "Amen!" Agreement seals their fates.

Patriarchal powers have crafted the marriage institution into one that women pursue and men flee from until successfully captured. This is because "femaleness is an entity dependent on maleness. . . . Yet maleness is not defined as a being related to woman but as a free being."[3] Women are groomed from the cradle to pant after marriage. Traditionally, marriage is a one-sided pursuit.

Scan your local newsstand. Notice that there are numerous brides' magazines. But are there any grooms' magazines? As a girl I played with Barbie dolls. My Barbie, and most others, made it her business to ensure that the Ken doll would marry her. It was expected, almost demanded. Marriage was the woman's and the girl's concern. It was our universal ideal. Marriage was the talk of girlhood. By the time I was ten years old, I'd planned my wedding down to the color scheme, music, and which aisle of the church I would march down. My friends and I dreamed of marrying any member of the singing group the Jackson Five. We romanticized and wished for that day with no idea what lay on the other side of the honeymoon.

The dreams of girls often grow into drama for women. Rita believed that she had to be married, and she rushed in at the first offer. Now she is stuck in the institution, and she knows it. Rigid gender roles rule her marriage to Eric. Those rules didn't seem real during the courtship. "It was all about getting the ring and getting married," Rita confessed. "I wanted a husband who was stable and reliable. He was all that and more. I did not notice it then, but he interprets the Bible literally," she explained. "He makes the rules and I follow. It seemed kind of romantic when we were dating. He was so strong and sure of himself. Now I see that it was a form of control. This is not what I planned on," Rita said.

Despite the casualties like Rita, sisters readily invest in the hope that a marrying kind of Prince Charming will come. "At least I got a man," they will be able to proclaim. But at what cost? The pursuit for the band of gold on the left hand has created a "marriage elitism" in churches. Marriage is an ideal state or "privileged position" in the Black church. It is exceedingly clear that marrying a (scarce) black man, especially one with at least some hint of religiosity, is a coup. Those sisters who have a man hold their heads a little higher than those who don't. Having a man is like having a license to enjoy life.

Not all women are rushing in. Statistics from the United States Census Bureau offer us a bleak but telling picture of women who are firmly rejecting the harness of marriage for the freedom of singlehood. Pregnancy is no longer a reason to marry. Most unmarried pregnant women choose not to marry before their child is born. And the face of America's families reflects this, as two-parent homes are odd, not common.[4] More women are discarding marriage due to its historic hassles and headaches. They are saying with their actions, "I can do bad all by myself."

## Overhauling Traditional Misunderstandings

Change is not just an option for marriage. Marriage *must* be overhauled or face extinction. Just as with singles, marriage is an arena that New Faith eagerly molds and shapes for this millennium. Flawed interpretations of the Scriptures have turned marriages into traps. We want love, but we reject suffering. We want commitment, but we do not want to return to slavery. We've come too far to turn back now. We've tasted freedom and equity in all other areas. Marriage will be no different.

I've seen Christian husbands and wives struggle for headship in marriages instead of pursuing collaboration. They claw and scrape their way into being the leader, when all the while Christ is the true leader. Over the years I've led many couples through premarital counseling sessions. They are forewarned that this is not the traditional type of premarital counseling. "I do not advocate domination," I caution them. "If you want to dominate someone, go get a dog; don't get married." I teach couples about communication, compromise, and collaboration. A sign on my office door is their first lesson. It reads, "Blessed are the flexible, for they shall not be bent out of shape."

Many couples come seeking rigid roles because they don't know any better. It is easier to mindlessly follow what they've seen and heard but never thought about. I vividly remember one particular couple who came quoting the Ephesians 5:22 text. The woman understood that she was to transfer all authority to her fiancé, but she was not happy about it. Her fiancé did not say it, but his body language conveyed his anxiety with the passage and its implications for their marriage. "What does the passage mean?" I asked them at our first session. "It means that I'm responsible for her, me, and everything," he said. "Everything! The strategies, the planning, the decisions, and all. That's a lot. I can barely keep up with myself," he confessed. "How will I do it all?" he asked as a tear trickled down his face. He was terrified of all the commitment and responsibility that was his and his alone. His fiancée comforted him, and I did, too. I said, "You don't have to. You can both shoulder the load." He looked up, smiled, and said, "Thank you."

Just as women are looking for the exit signs away from traditional marriage, men are looking for ways to shift or share the responsibility. The images of marriage as presented in Scripture are often in conflict. There is domination and even domestic violence. And there is equality and partnership. Understandably this has caused ambivalence, and downright confusion exists in Christian homes. There are basically two schools of thought: traditional marriage and partnership marriage. Both viewpoints look at the same Scripture passages and interpret them differently. Let's look at both.

> And the Lord God said, "It is not good that the man should be alone; I will make a helper fit for him." (Gen. 2:18)

Traditionalists suggest that this passage means that God created woman after man because her role was to assist him, not lead or co-lead.

> Your desire shall be for your husband, and he shall rule over you. (Gen. 3:16)

Traditionalists suggest that this passage establishes God's order for the home. The husband is the ruler.

> Wives, be subject to your husbands, as to the Lord. For the husband is the head of the wife as Christ is the head of the church, his body, and is himself its Savior. As the church is subject to Christ, so let wives also be subject in everything to their husbands. Husbands, love your wives, as Christ loved the church and gave himself up for her, that he might sanctify her, having cleansed her by the washing of water with the word, that he might present the church to himself in splendor, without spot or wrinkle or any such thing, that she might be holy and without blemish. Even so husbands should love their wives as their own bodies. He who loves his wife loves himself. For no man ever hates his own flesh, but nourishes and cherishes it, as Christ does the church, because we are members of his body. (Eph. 5:22-31)

Here traditionalists tell us that the husband is the biblical ruler and that he has the final word and governs all family affairs. He is to rule her with great love. According to one traditionalist, "No woman in her right mind resists placing

herself willingly and submissively under a man who loves
her as Christ loved the church."[5]

> Likewise you wives, be submissive to your husbands,
> so that some, though they do not obey the word, may
> be won without a word by the behavior of their
> wives, when they see your reverent and chaste
> behavior. Let not yours be the outward adorning
> with braiding of hair, decoration of gold, and wear-
> ing of fine clothing, but let it be the hidden person of
> the heart with the imperishable jewel of a gentle and
> quiet spirit, which in God's sight is very precious. So
> once the holy women who hoped in God used to
> adorn themselves and were submissive to their hus-
> bands, as Sarah obeyed Abraham, calling him lord.
> And you are now her children if you do right and let
> nothing terrify you. Likewise you husbands, live con-
> siderately with your wives, bestowing honor on the
> woman as the weaker sex, since you are joint heirs of
> the grace of life, in order that your prayers may not
> be hindered. (1 Pet. 3:1-7)

Traditionalists say that this passage indicates that women
are obviously the weaker vessel and must follow the hierarchy in marriage that places the husbands over them as
their masters.

In some traditional marriages the literal interpretations
strangle the couple's abilities to function. The marriage of
Bill and Brenda is an example of the unnecessary suffering that comes from the flawed interpretations. Both of
these faithful, Bible-quoting churchgoers are business
owners. Bill operates a lawn maintenance company, and
Brenda is a tailor. By day they are capable and successful
entrepreneurs. By night Brenda must release her compe-
tency to live the role of the traditional submissive wife.
She struggles to serve God and to be the woman that God
created her to be. She is frustrated, confused, and angry.
"All day long I can think, organize, and manage my business, but as soon as I set foot in the door I have to stop
thinking," she snapped. "How in the world do I turn off

and turn on my assertive, competitive nature? Is it ungodly for me to have an opinion?" she asked.

## Roots of the Domination Fixation

The clash between strong-willed, assertive sisters and the brothers who wish they would sit down and shut up is growing louder, as more of us ask, Why must I sit down and shut up? It is a fact that African American women would not have survived without our sass, fire, and backbone. These three elements are our coping kit for life. To suggest that in order to please men we must abandon what has brought us this far is ludicrous. Rather, New Faith searches for the roots of man's desperate need to dominate women.

Our theologian sister Dr. Renita Weems marvelously uncovers the biblical history. She makes it clear that the domination fixation is neither natural nor godly. She explains that it originated from a metaphor or image of God's relationship with Israel that was based on the relationship between a husband and a wife. Old Testament prophets Ezekiel, Hosea, and Jeremiah needed a vehicle that aptly described the way God felt about God's people, and the image of marriage captured their imagination. By using the marriage metaphor, "a whole range of behavior associated with intimacy and mating was brought to mind."[6] She writes: "The advantage of the marriage metaphor in casting Israel as a woman was its ability to construe Israel's behavior not simply as rebellion or immaturity, but as depravity and shamelessness. . . . It also called upon a male honor system where a man's prestige rested in great part on his ability to control the behavior of the subordinates in his household (e.g., wives, slaves, children)."[7]

Thus the Scriptures present God as a controlling, dominating husband and Israel as the wild wife in need of domination. In Ezekiel 16:35 the husband demonstrates his power to call his wife names and condemn her. "Therefore, O whore, hear the word of the LORD: thus says the Lord GOD, Because your lust was poured out and your nakedness uncovered in your whoring with your lovers, and because of all your abominable idols . . ." (NRSV). In Hosea 2:2 there is the image of a betrayed, angry husband retaliating against his guilty wife: ". . . for she is not my wife, and I am not her husband—that she put away her harlotry from her face, and her adultery from between her breasts; lest I strip her naked. . . ." In Jeremiah 4:30 the reader experiences a husband's control of his wife's attire and self-esteem. "And you, O desolate one, what do you mean that you dress in scarlet, that you deck yourself with ornaments of gold, that you enlarge your eyes with paint? In vain you beautify yourself."

Weems continues: "The metaphor was not interested, as some have supposed, in stressing romance, intimacy, and mutuality. Rather, the metaphor focused on belittling female judgment and condemning the wife as fickle, untrustworthy, loose, and stubborn. At the same time, the metaphor elevated the husband to the position of noble benefactor, innocent of any wrongdoing."[8] Weems concludes that this metaphor is based on an assumption of men's power over women's sexuality and reflects men's fascination with female nakedness. From this perspective, men's activities are analogous to God's actions. Weems theorizes that the metaphor was created from a man's perspective for the male imagination.[9]

The desire to control the women and attain honor from that control carried over from the Old Testament and into the New Testament, as noted in the Roman Household codes, which gave husbands legal power over their wives. New Faith urges us to notice that Jesus did not uphold Roman household codes. He did not subjugate women. For example, he stood against the sexist tide by defending and defusing the anger against the woman caught in adultery (John 8:4). The group wanted her stoned. They'd lost control of her sexuality. Jesus turned the table on them and asked which of them had a clean life. "Let him who is without sin among you be the first to throw a stone at her" (John 8:7).

### Authentic Intimacy

New Faith looks at the Scriptures regarding marriage with the conviction that Jesus, who ultimately defined the role of women, also defines marriage. "The Jesus of the Gospels approaches women directly as disciples, so that their religious identity does not depend on their fathers and husbands or being married or having children."[10] New Faith also asks the hard questions about these infamous passages. If Paul wanted women to submit and live under the authority of their husbands, why did he declare that men and women were equal in Galatians 3:28? Or why do traditionalists take some parts of Scripture literally but ignore other parts? Today we regard slavery as an antiquated offensive institution. Today Paul's reference to the accommodation to slavery is dismissed automatically: "Slaves, obey in everything those who are your earthly masters, not with eyeservice, as men-pleasers, but in singleness of heart, fearing the Lord" (Col. 3:22). Why can't we see that the submission of women is equally an antiquated offensive institution as slavery?

In the Genesis 2:18-24 passage, those who propose partnership marriages suggest that the key to equality is found in the translation of the word "help." "The words *help* and *meet* in the King James Version translate two Hebrew words, *ezer* and *neged*. The word *ezer* ('help') is never used in the Bible to refer to a subordinate helper but is used in reference to God as our Helper as in Psalms 121:1,2. The word *neged* is a preposition in Hebrew, but the most accurate way to translate it into English is by giving it a meaning such as 'corresponding to.' . . . The idea is that Eve was an appropriate, fitting partner for Adam."[11]

As for the Genesis 3:16 passage, those who propose partnership marriages tell us that "God is not here issuing a special commandment. But . . . we have a statement, a prediction, a prophecy, of how man, degenerated by sin, would take advantage of his headship as husband to dominate, lord it over, his wife." Curiously, the sentence that follows, which condemns man to thorn and thistle, is not adhered to in our society. Rather "herbicides, air conditioning and other devices"[12] compensate. If we take the Scriptures literally, it dictates that the agriculture work should be limited to thorn and thistle. Why are we loosely translating here but literally translating elsewhere?

In interpreting Ephesians 5, those supporting partnership marriage point to Ephesians 5:21, "Submit to one another as to Christ," which is often overlooked. This call for mutual submission found there actually describes the ideal intimate marriage. When we submit to each other, our marriages have a mutuality that removes the pressure of sole control.

The cultural context of the Scriptures must be taken into account. The Roman law of *Patria Potestas* held the husband responsible for the conduct of his wife; he was amenable for her offenses.[13] "Roman law made the husband the sole head of his wife."[14] Those who advocate partnership marriages suggest that husbands do not "dominate their wives, but minister to them, as Christ ministers to the church."[15] A woman might greatly desire to see her husband converted but have little power to influence him in religious matters.[16]

Partnership marriages do not advocate that the wife address her husband with the lofty title of "Lord," as stated in verse 6. "The word usually rendered 'lord' or 'master' is better translated 'sir,' for it was a term of respect, not servitude."[17] The reference to braids and gold jewelry especially hits home in the African American churches, as many, many of us wear braids and drape our bodies with gold necklaces, earrings, and bracelets. If we seek to follow the Scriptures letter for letter, we would see that submitting also includes unbraiding our hair and removing the gold from our bodies. If nothing else wakes us up, this should show us that literalism is haphazardly applied to women and harmful to us.

## Partnership Marriage

I have been in a partnership marriage with my husband Robert for fifteen years. I have not been forced to surrender myself. Rather, through the partnership, I have found more of me. My aspirations soar, my individuality is not compromised, and my mind still functions. I am proof that we can share and give ourselves over to a marriage and not lose ourselves, silence ourselves, or minimize our spunk. But it is not easy. It requires vigilance to maintain self while becoming one flesh. We must retain our original selves in collaboration with another. The historical temptation is to forget self and cling to him, or deny self and lavish him. Maintaining self is a daily challenge that I relish because the survival of me in the marriage is crucial. Without me there is only him, and without him there is not a marriage. I've discovered that marriage is not akin to erasing what was and starting over. I must constantly monitor myself, my boundaries, my beliefs, my habits, and my practices to ensure that they are still my own. If the original self enters the marriage weak, then the marriage may be fragile. Real men relish women with independent thoughts, ideas, plans, and dreams.

New Faith shatters the old myths that being married means being taken care of. Sisters must enter marriage with their eyes wide open. Marriage is work seven days a week, twenty-four hours a day. Marriage is not a playground. Marriage is not like the cruise control of a car; it requires constant vigilance. I work hard to be caring, considerate, compassionate, and communicative with my spouse—even when I don't feel like it. I deserve a paycheck every Friday. I am a New Faith wife. My marriage strives for oneness. I pray that more sisters will join me. Allow me to share a few more recommendations for marriage.

*1. New Faith wives don't expect their husbands to make them happy.* This is not the husband's job. He is not responsible for their joy. Married women should ensure that their needs are being met.

Sandra is sitting around waiting on her husband to meet her needs. She is growing tired of tarrying. She'd like to go on walks in the evenings after work, but he doesn't want to, so they don't. She'd like a diamond bracelet, but he does not want to buy it. She does not get one. Sandra never thought about going on walks by herself or using some of her own money to purchase a bracelet. Such acts would not convey a lack of love for her husband but rather a strong love of self. She needs to love herself enough to make herself happy. That's not her husband's job.

*2. New Faith wives learn to enjoy marital sex.* They have overcome the mental and emotional barricades built by premarital sex guilt. Years of threats from momma, daddy, and the preacher not to let boys get in our pants have constructed mental obstacles to sexual pleasure. "Just don't do it" is emblazoned in our minds. It can be difficult to switch mental gears, and some Christian women have difficulty enjoying sex with their husbands. "If it was 'the nasty' before we were married, how is the same sex with the same man now different?" one woman asked. "The difference," I explained, "is that the devil seeks to rob marriage of the joys of sexual intimacy, while he ensures that the single community enjoys it. We've got to take back what belongs to marriage."

*3. New Faith wives understand that our tongues are considered lethal weapons.* If you catch a sister at the wrong time, she can easily and effortlessly slice and dice a man to bits in seconds with razor-sharp words, inflections, and posture. New Faith wives recognize this innate ability and speak to our spouses with kindness. Our tone of voice should encourage him and lift him up.

Veronique was known for neck-working, finger-pointing, and eyeball-rolling. She knew this was comical at the appropriate times but lethal for her marriage. "I've learned to think before I speak or move a muscle," she shared. "Before I open my mouth I ask myself, are my comments helpful or hurtful to the marriage?"

4. *New Faith wives know all there is to know about the money in their home.* We need to know about household income, bills, insurance policies, Certificates of Deposit, 401(k)s, and all other money situations. Knowledge is power, and money is power, too. Love is not blind or naive.

None of us can forget the classic scene from the movie *Waiting to Exhale* when sister discovers that her husband, whom she trusted and loved, had hidden millions and was planning to dump her for a younger woman. She was hurt, angry, betrayed, and humiliated. Don't let this happen to you. Review the mail, ask questions, and get the information you need.

5. *New Faith wives take seriously the threat of adultery* and don't place themselves in compromising positions with men. The sacredness of our oneness means protecting yourself from temptation. Don't overestimate your ability to resist seduction. It is a strong force.

Celeste thought she had an affair-proof marriage. She had a husband who loved her, and she loved him. And then a male co-worker began to compliment her hair and wardrobe. He listened to her and supported her ideas. He supplied her with what she missed at home, and a sexual relationship developed between them. Before she realized what she was doing, Celeste was in an affair with her co-worker. Eventually her husband found out. He asked why, and all she could say was, "I didn't mean to do it. It just happened."

Yes, we are working for a oneness in marriage. Marriage looks good from the perspective of New Faith. We have reviewed the Scriptures and the cultural contexts. Marriage was never meant to be a ball and chain. It is a partnership. It is an investment of ideas, emotion, and intimacy. Our men are worth it. Of course we are worth it. We will be free to be who Jesus says we are in marriage. Any other way snatches us back to what was, and we ain't marching in reverse.

## Reflection Questions

1. What has traditional marriage cost us?
2. Is submission necessary in light of New Faith?
3. How can the church end the "domination fixation"?
4. Should wives be responsible for their own happiness?

# Cleaning Up the House

"... light a lamp and sweep the house." (Luke 15:8)

**New Faith works** if you work it. Sisters, now is the time to work it as we've never worked it before. Personal action is requested, required, and highly recommended. We can read all the books in the bookstore, pray the day away, and meditate till the next millennium comes, but if we do not act, we squander the tears of those who came before us. Faith with no legs is a waste of time. Our legs have brought us so remarkably far, so beautifully far, that rest is not on our agenda. The work before us is housecleaning. We must clean up the church house. If we sweep, dust, vacuum, do the laundry, sanitize, and mop in a New Faith rhythm, our results will be righteous, and the church will finally reflect the true nature of God.

New Faith instructs us to clean up the house with order and purpose like the woman of Luke 15:8 swept, mopped, and dusted her entire house. First she lit a lamp to see what needed to be done. Our efforts thus far of educating and inspiring are the illumination needed. The dark shadows of resistance are dissipating.

The woman in Luke also knew what she was looking for. She was looking for her lost coin. We are looking for something, too—the dissolution of patriarchal Christianity and the establishment of parity in the pulpit and the pews. Cleaning with a goal in mind is the only way to clean. It is a new way to clean. Who would mindlessly clean up? We would! For centuries we have ceremonially and perfunctorily rearranged the dust, grime, and soot because we knew it wasn't going anywhere. It was unthinkable. Our cleaning solvents were given to us by the patriarchs and thus designed not to disinfect, but to disorient us. It was a part of the historical church game. We were pawns who were played. Even today, "many of us think and act as though it's 'natural' if not 'normal' for men to dominate."[1] Sadly this strongly held concept "gives rise to universal male authority over women and a higher valuation of male over female roles."[2]

We should know better. We are better than that. We are not pitiful; we are powerful. We are sagacious, shrewd, and sharp housecleaners who actually function as house revolutionaries. We revolutionaries do not "wish to destroy the house of authority. Quite the contrary, we wish to build it up again as a new house"[3] of New Faith. The responsibility to redirect the church rests on our shoulders. No one but us will rescue us. The Lord helps those who help themselves. Cleaning is what we do well: Most of us know our way around a mop, a broom, and a bucket. It is our way out and up.

It is vital that we agree and understand that our task is not a piecemeal project. We are cleaning the entire house—every room, top to bottom, the choir loft to the pastor's study—in order to enact a paradigm shift. It is not enough for individuals to do their best; systems must change as well. We seek complete overhaul of the African American church—the thinking, the working, the processing, and the planning. The only untouchable and unchangeable is Jesus, God, and the Holy Spirit.

Let me put that more plainly. "When we work at things piece by piece, we do not necessarily change structures of thought used for interpretation, preaching, and Christian life. It is a little like trying to win Monopoly when you just own Baltic Avenue without any hotels."[4] We seek to change the entire system, not just one church or one section of town.

It is vital that all women clean up. This is not a spectator sport. We face an uphill battle when we attempt to rally all the troops. Patriarchy is not a heinous villain to every woman. Religious sexism "is so integrated into our lives and our institutions that it becomes like breathing— present until we die."[5] Some sisters will reject my thesis that brands sexist suffering as unnecessary because they don't feel oppressed. "I love my church. I love my pastor. I love the Lord. I ain't changing nothing," some will say. "Nobody has done anything wrong to me. I don't see the problem," others will reply.

The truth is, "one can be oppressed without feeling oppressed. The litmus test for whether or not oppression is indeed happening may not necessarily be those to whom it is happening. Our human ability for denial and obfuscation cannot be underestimated as both are a tool for self-preservation and a means for continued domination and subjugation."[6]

Also there will be sisters who choose not to clean up the house because they are beneficiaries of the church status quo. They profit from the patriarchy. "A woman who experiences a measure of comfort and security must work with great diligence to uncover the sharp double edge of oppression and domination."[7] Such sisters will be the most unlikely to join us, yet they can effect the most change.

Here is our church-cleaning strategy: The first cleaning to be done is among us; second there is cleaning that only our men can do; and last there is cleaning that only can occur when we join with our men—in true womanist fashion—to clean the house together.

## Women's Work
### Speak up

Cleaning up means church women speak up. You've thought it, but you held the thought inside. Either there was no one to tell or no one cared. And besides, women who point out problems are troublemakers. When we talked, trouble came our way. "Speech against structures creates change. Silence does not."[8] We have not been taken seriously for so long we stopped speaking. Long ago, "in seventeenth-century America, a woman who spoke out in public could expect to be bound to a dunking stool and submerged under water. When she was brought up, gasping for air, she was offered the choice between silence or drowning."[9]

"I've been holding my tongue for thirty years," Sister Delores admitted quietly. This mother of the church had wanted to offer constructive criticism about her church to the pastor and male deacons but never did. "I worried what would happen to me. It's clear that church women don't do a lot of talking; we are the doers," she said. "It's easier if I just keep quiet." There are millions of Sister Deloreses out there. They sit there with a smile and an "Amen," and it is assumed that they are happy.

### Cease the competition

Cleaning up means women will reassess our thoughts of each other. "Often we do not realize that the black woman we see as competing with us or treating us with disregard may be in need of sisterly care and recognition. If we cannot look past the surface and see what lies underneath we will not be able to give one another the compassionate understanding we also need in our daily lives."[10]

The automatic putdowns and slurs flow from our mouths like water. When Sister Beckwith walked down the aisle to join church on Sunday, the heads of the church hens began to wag. "Humph. She thinks she's cute. I can tell by the way she holds her head," sneered one. "I bet she was wearing a weave," said another. "And wonder where did she get that tired pink suit?" a third queried.

Why are we so quick to jump at each other's throats? One researcher put it best by saying, "competition is always present between women. The nature of subordinance produces dysfunctional competition between the one-down people—competition for resources, love, approval, and help from dominants."[11]

In the Black church where we do not have an equal share of the power, we rely on men, and "when a woman relies on a man for her livelihood, she must always make sure that another woman does not take him away. Her one-down position carries inherent competition with other women."[12]

### Legitimize women's ways of working

Cleaning up means we remove the dust that blinded our eyes to our greatness. Women's ways of working are different. Historically, "different" was wrong, inferior, and embarrassing. Yet God made us the way we are. New Faith says we lead with our strengths and not our weaknesses. This is our form of legitimizing or approving ourselves. This is not a putdown of what is male. Rather, we salute what the Lord has done.

Sylvia always knew she was a leader. Back in the day she coalesced all the kids on the block of her neighborhood. "I had them unified in everything from civic projects to Easter plays. I never knew why I could, I just could," she reflected. And even now she brings the members of her church together in ways that defy explanation. She doesn't raise her voice or stand up and wave her arms; she just has something that makes them follow. It's called women's ways. There are four prominent ways of working common to us. Let's recognize and celebrate them.

- Participatory management: Women have "the willingness to spend time with people creating a win-win situation."[13] Women have learned how to collaborate and that means I get something, you get something, and we all get something in return.
- Willingness to share information: "Women don't see leadership as having to have all the answers and be an expert."[14] It's O.K. to ask, seek another's opinion, and be vulnerable to another's ideas.
- Concern for human relationships: It matters to us how Sister Brown feels about us. We are relational creatures, and we can't help ourselves. Women "bring a more relational approach to leadership."[15]
- Ability to do many things at once: We established early in this book that women are multi-taskers. There is no shame in fixing dinner, combing a head, and preparing Bible study simultaneously. "By virtue of their life experiences, women are able to do many more things at once."[16]

### Understand power

Cleaning up means we will look at power with New Faith eyes. Our fear or even disgust will diminish with this focus. I loathed power because I had been manhandled by it. The wounds inflicted by power made me nauseous at the thought of using it against others. When power fell into my lap as senior pastor, I was confused and clueless. It was years before I learned that there are two kinds of power, and they are both good. There is power as commodity and power as relationship. Power as a commodity is "power over," the authoritative power that is so often exhibited by oppressive males. Power as relationship is "power with" and usually favored by women. It is based on the interaction of people and organizations to accomplish its end.

Each of these forms of power is legitimate and useful. It was easy to use "power with" in the company of women, but I needed both types. I needed the "power over" to make my presence felt and carry out my authority. I had to understand that I deserved this ability. Power over is not evil, inappropriate, or destructive unless it is abused. Women fall into a trap when they believe otherwise.

### Stop deferring and lead something
Cleaning up will mean church women will take the lead—sometimes. Deferring is an ingrained impediment that New Faith surgically removes. I've seen it time after time: The qualified sister and the qualified brother are offered leadership roles, and the sister instinctively defers, as if it's a sin to lead and to supersede a Black man at anything. We dismiss the notion that their egos must be protected at our loss. "We are so quick to put ourselves in the servant role that we do not always recognize and use the power we already have. Too often we get duped into giving it away."[17] We are too eager to bake the pie and not chair the meeting.

### Be a mentor
Cleaning up means we church women must release our insecurities and open doors for each other. There a few things more pathetic than a sister at the top who smashes the stretched hands of other women struggling upward, trying to follow her. Church women must be mentors and opportunity providers for each other. The bright glare of attention that comes from being the first woman to do

such and such in the church can be intoxicating. Don't be a first too long. Share the spotlight with another woman as soon as possible.

We must understand that the power we seek sometimes comes by invitation only—our invitation. "Women mistakenly believe that professional preparation is the only criterion for promotion or that hard work is always rewarded, for both men and women."[18] Mentors help "them gain the necessary clout for upward mobility, developing leadership skills, and accessibility to other decision makers."[19]

Female mentors are also essential because in some instances male mentors do not "understand the rules of professional conduct for women."[20] There have been many times when I've been in the presence of "great and revered" clergymen. I stood in their presence along with a throng of male clergy. But there was a distinct boys' club feel there that I could not penetrate, no matter how long I stood with them. Eventually, the circle around the clergyman tightened, and I was excluded. Those men may have approved of me, but I was not a man and could not come into their inner circle. I yearned to laugh at their jokes and hear the pulpit exploits but could not. I was a woman. The invaluable advice was off-limits.

### Endorse clergywomen

Cleaning up means enlarging the concept of pastor to include women. Narrow-mindedness in this area hurts church womanhood more intensely than any other. Clergywomen-hating church women are ubiquitous and ever ready to cut down, thwart, and hinder God's movement through women. I choose to forget the depths of their self-hate, and I am always caught off guard when such a sister strikes. "It's bad enough that she is a woman, but she is a Methodist too!" was the slur. "A woman can't teach me anything or lead me anywhere" was another.

Women's comments can be the most hurtful, because change cannot come until we accept one another.

According to prominent pastor Dr. Vashti M. McKenzie, clergywomen are held to a different, more severe standard:

> If she is too good looking, she is regarded suspiciously by other women and men. If she is committed to her ministry, then she must be unhappy at home. If she balances her work and home life, then she is neglecting her "call." If she looks too glamorous, then she is looking for extra male companionship. If she does not look glamorous at all, she has no self-pride. If she dresses too well or lives too "high on the hog," then she must be stealing. If she does not live well enough, she is an embarrassment to God and the church. If she is single, then she must be scouting the congregation for a husband. If she is a married woman, she must be either playing the field or not taking care of her husband and children properly.[21]

## Balance private and church self

Cleaning up means church women will learn that serving the Lord does not mean sacrificing self. The days of being the long-suffering, spread-thin, drained church woman are over. We've got to find the healthy balance between church, family, and self. There is always at least one sister in the church who is perched on the front steps every time the doors open. You know her.

"Girl, I am busy for the Lord," she brays, searching for sympathy and adoration. "I've got choir practice on Monday night, mission board on Tuesday night, Bible study on Wednesday night, drill team on Thursday night, singles on Friday night, and on Saturday we evangelize the neighborhood."

Some whisper to themselves, "Does she have a cot in the church basement?" "Does she have a life?" I ask. Being at the church every night of the week for meetings, rehearsals, and so on is not wise. Overextension is not what God wants from us. Serving on multiple committees can be a form of escapism from problematic people, places, or things.

**Realize that the pastor is human**

Cleaning up means that we wash away the myth that the pastor is perfect. He is not a god, never has been, and never will be. In some churches the pastor is placed on a pedestal and kept there by the people. Women put him there in a desperate search for a decent Black man. Up on the pedestal, he has no boundaries or accountability and is a victim of our adoration. He is incapable of sins and mistakes. This is a dangerous environment, especially for women, because such flawed leadership will be covered up and the victim will be blamed.

> When Pastor Clark's hand swiped Sister Jones' breast for the second time during their counseling session, she'd had enough. The first time may have been an accident but the second time was intentional. "I don't play that!" declared the forty-five-year-old accountant. She stormed out of his office, down the hall, and into the deacon's meeting room. She gave an account of the sexual misconduct to the men gathered. Little did she know she'd entered a twilight zone of sorts where the reality is ignored and fantasy reigns. The deacons barely glanced up from their meeting table as she spoke. Once she left, her words evaporated from their minds like fresh rain on hot pavement.[22]

## Men's Work

Men who support New Faith are housecleaners too. We welcome their assistance. They understand that it is not just women's work. Our men can reach nooks and crannies that we can't. They want to see a paradigm shift. They want to share power.

**Listen to women**

Men can clean up by listening—no talking, just listening. Their silence removes the barriers that have kept us mute.

Their silence gives us an inch to get a word in and allows us to be heard. Their silence confirms that they don't know it all and demonstrates their willingness to participate in mutual submission. "Men cannot know what we want and what the possibilities are unless they listen."[23] "It's going to be hard for them. In a way, women are at an advantage when listening is required. We already know their world and their way of doing things. We have to. But they don't know us very well."[24]

Listening to a woman is the first major step for many men who considered it heretical for a woman to tell them anything. The day that Reverend Magee listened to the women of his church was monumental. All five of the women who petitioned him for membership on the deacon's board desperately wanted his ear. He "allowed" them each to speak, get feelings off their chests, and share their experiences. It was difficult, but he sat still and listened. The longer he listened, the more he learned about the women, about the church, and about life. Once the women finished speaking, Reverend Magee breathed a sigh of relief and thought to himself, "That wasn't too bad. I even learned something."

## Set the tone of acceptance

Cleaning up means that men physically and figuratively open the church door to the acceptance of women. Specifically, men must ". . . affirm what women do, advocate women in leadership, don't label family concessions of the workplace women's issues, help women advance."[25] Men must include women in the decisions and bring them to the table early, not as an afterthought. The hierarchy of the patriarchy dictates that men set the tone. Some people will wait and watch to see what the pastor and other men do and follow them and only them. Therefore men will set the tone for our ascent. If the pastor says it's O.K., it must be O.K. If the brethren say it's all right, it must be all right.

This reality surfaced when I preached at a men's retreat for a conservative Baptist Church. The men eyed me suspiciously prior to my address because they did not know what would happen. The men were not certain how to receive me. They needed direct guidance. Even though the senior pastor had personally invited me by letter and by follow-up phone call, he realized that he needed to smooth my pathway a little more. When I stepped toward the pulpit to preach, he suddenly leaped up ahead of me and introduced me again to his men. He added, "Brothers, she's alright; hear her gladly." Immediately the strained mood of the men was lifted from the auditorium and the men relaxed, and completely received my sermon. The men just needed his permission.

### Confess sexism in the church

Men can clean up the church by telling the truth about sexism. Confession is good for the soul. Sexism allows men to "do all the talking, and to believe that they are more competent than women on most things, regardless of their experience."[26] This lie has discolored the church from the beginning. We've pretended, ignored, and turned away from this evil giant long enough.

"Men of color have an obligation to extract from their eyes the lens of sexism through which they view the world, no less than white men have an obligation to remove the lens of racism through which they view the world."[27] This evil must be publicly decried if there is to be change. There are women waiting for this admission, which will heal old wounds. When women have asked that sexism be named, friction occurs. "In those rare instances where serious questions are raised against misogynistic assumptions, presumptions, and practices (such as women being capable of preparing but not distributing communion), the questioner, if female, is denounced as a man-hater, if male, as a dominated wimp."[28]

# What We Can Do Together

## Desexualize the church

Only together can men and women clean away this stubborn stain on the church. Sex is power, and the power of the Black church is held tightly by the patriarchy. Power is the aphrodisiac that draws women to the men. Church life encourages women to pursue this power at any cost.

The Black church is a sexual powder keg because "there is an erotic power in the pulpit. For generations men have benefited from the attention, flattery and gifts given them by women in their congregation."[29] When the erotic nature of the male-dominated pulpit ignites the sexually charged pews full of women, explosions occur. Usually we are victimized by the "Madonna/whore syndrome":

> The Madonna most frequently is noted on Mother's Day when the woman in the congregation who has borne the greatest number of children (with benefit of wedlock) is singled out for recognition. The whore is identified primarily in relation to the number of men in the congregation who either actually or allegedly have had sex with her. A woman's place in this seemingly polarized arena is subject to shifting arbitrarily as she engages in behavior deemed worthy of praise or blame.[30]

Together men and women of the church can decrease the sexual tension by sharing the power and freeing women from rigid gender roles.

## Use inclusive language

Cleaning up together means we can find room for other ways of speaking about God. This openness will bring down barriers that have kept women feeling spiritually small and less-than. Words have tremendous power. For example, one of the most common church words is *man*. Are females subsumed within references to *man, mankind,* and *he*? Although the word *man* has been used for centuries as if it were generic, women and men furrow their brows when they hear "the sisterhood of women. . . . By using more inclusive words such as human beings or women and men, we can be sure everyone is included."[31]

Yes, it will cause Deacon Brogan to have a hissy, but God is more than a human gender. Let's not ignore the realities of God. We do not need to throw out the traditional masculine language, but there is room in our brains for more.

## Preach to include all

Cleaning up the church together means that the sacred art of homiletics must also be purged. Sermons are the most anticipated portion of the worship service. We have some of the most gifted men and women of God standing in our pulpits. Their words preach us happy. If New Faith is to heal us, however, we need to ask the following questions of even the most stirring messages: Do illustrations in sermons refer to women and men only in stereotypical social roles? Do interpretations of Scriptures ever focus on the positive roles of women in Bible stories? Daniel, Hosea, and Gideon are flush preaching material, but so are Deborah, Mary, and Esther.

## Protect the progress

Cleaning up together means we must protect what we have built. In-house watchdog/advocacy groups keep us honest and focused on our goal of equity. Otherwise we stray or lose our enthusiasm.

> We must continually review this commitment and evaluate whether or not it's being energized by effective thought or action. Researchers have found that groups committed to egalitarian relationships among women and men fall back into old communication patterns that undermine their commitment, but when groups remind themselves periodically of their commitment and review their communication, they

are able to sustain healthier, more egalitarian patterns of communication.[32]

Such commissions would do well to set in place church-related sexual-harassment policies and even gender-sensitivity classes.

### Affect colleges and seminaries

Our joint cleaning can have far-reaching effects if we extend our touch beyond the stained-glass walls.

> The teaching of "egalitarianism" in gender-inclusive curriculum for colleges and seminaries is a must. This curriculum is sensitive to and elevates the contributions of women in church history, the development of theological thought, biblical hermeneutics, leadership, and homiletics. . . .[33]

Housecleaning is a specialty of Jesus, too. In Matthew 21:12, he cleaned up the temple, which teemed with inappropriate behavior. That's the other cleaning image I want you to see as well. He came and saw that the church was out of order. He got busy. We must also. We are a mighty cleaning force. We are united with our brothers and ourselves; we are a team in the name of Jesus. I predict success, just like the cleaning woman found in Luke. When she finds what she was looking for, "'she calls together her friends and neighbors, saying, "Rejoice with me, for I have found the coin which I had lost." . . .'" (Luke 15:9). Like her, we will rejoice when we find what we seek. Only then can the party begin. What a party it will be!

## Reflection Questions

1. Can you become a house revolutionary?
2. What is your understanding of power?
3. Have you noticed the sexual undertones of worship services?
4. Will inclusive language help clean up the church?

# 12 Striving toward the Vision

"'Write the vision; make it plain on tablets, so that a runner may read it. For there is still a vision for the appointed time; it speaks of the end, and does not lie. If it seems to tarry, wait for it; it will surely come, it will not delay." (Habakkuk 2:2-3 NRSV)

**M**y counter-cultural strut has accelerated into a stride, and now I am sprinting toward what the Lord has for me. That's the only way to get there—seize it, grab it, so that it won't escape my reach. The forward motion shall never cease. I fear if I stop pressing on, the momentum will end. If I stop moving, I fear that the time of ignorance and oppression will resume, and I will end up as just another restricted Black woman in somebody's church (plantation), worshipping a God I neither love, nor fear, nor understand.

Movement is the key. When I'm moving, I can feel the pulse of God and I can sense the strength that God provides. (Maybe it's also because a moving target is harder to hit.) In motion I dared to cast my vision before you. Some will be able to move with me, while others will falter and fade back into what was. Still I cast a vision. In Habakkuk the Lord instructs the prophets to record the vision. That is a risky thing. Vision writers take risks.

This book has been a vulnerable movement of my soul, because on the pages I opened up and poured out. I've shared personal and private thoughts because the truth must be shared. I praise God for the freedom to release what God birthed in me. Some people will read this book and declare, "See, I told you she was crazy." Others will snort, "I told you she hated men." I pray that the greater numbers of readers will cry out with joy, "Thank God for the truth."

The vision that I cast is of braver, wiser church women. They will no longer be victims of the church. The spoon-fed religion of the past will never do, not in this millennium. Womanist thought will be commonplace. The sisters will interpret the Scriptures for themselves and theologize about God from their understanding. They will do all of this with the same flair they have for cooking, dressing, and communicating. Conversations after church will never be the same. "Girl, what did you think about the eschatology of the sermon?" one will ask. "I felt it was strong, especially in the doctrine of salvation," another will reply.

Sisters will understand God and will also understand and value themselves. When every African American woman comes to understand that she is worth at least $500 billion dollars on a bad day, she will comprehend who she is in God. An unshakable, unbreakable self-love will flow forth, and depression levels will drop because we see who we are. Suicide will decrease because life has options.

Sisters will love themselves and love each other as sisters. Mentorship, partnership, and cooperation will replace the catty, viperous nature of church women. Rather than clawing up a wounded woman, the sisters will rally around her, bind up her wounds, and nurse her back to health, 'cause that's what sisters do.

Sisters will unite, join hands, and bravely clean up the Black church with a love that corrects and embraces simultaneously. The sisters love the Black church too much to leave it in a patriarchal state, because there is a more excellent way. The leadership, language, and literature of worship will reflect the presence and power of sisters as well as brothers.

Sisters will love their men without losing themselves. The needless suffering common to relationships will cease. Sisters will understand that being in love does not mean giving away self. And as a result, divorce rates will decrease because women will marry not out of desperation or fear but out of an understanding of unity in Christ. Dating for single women will not be as treacherous because they will have no tolerance for the games, lies, and deceit.

This vision will come to pass. It will not fail. Though it tarries, I will wait for it.

Concluding is never easy for me. I prefer to keep going and going and going. Although the book is ended, New Faith has not. New Faith cannot. There can be no end to our freedom process. We will keep on moving forward.

### Reflection Questions
1. Do you share the vision to change the Black church?
2. Will you interpret the Scriptures for yourself?
3. Will you love other women as your sisters?
4. Will you value yourself?
5. Will you love men without losing yourself?
6. Are you willing to begin moving forward?

# Notes

## 2. What Is New Faith?

1. Carol Saussy, *God Images and Self-Esteem* (Louisville, Ky.: Westminster/John Knox Press, 1991) 54.

2. Jacquelyn Grant, *White Woman's Christ and Black Woman's Jesus* (Atlanta: Scholars Press, 1989), 210.

3. Sheron C. Patterson, *Single Principles: The Single Woman's 10 Step Guide to Power* (Dallas: Perseverance Press, 1997) 70.

4. Gayraud S. Wilmore and James H. Cone, eds., *Black Theology: A Documentary History, 1966–1979* (Maryknoll, N.Y.: Orbis Books, 1979) 423.

5. Emilie Townes, ed., *A Troubling in My Soul: Womanist Perspectives on Evil and Suffering* (Maryknoll, N.Y.: Orbis Books, 1993) 41.

6. Vashti M. McKenzie, *Not without a Struggle: Leadership Development for African American Women in Ministry* (Cleveland: United Church Press, 1996) 36.

7. Ibid.

8. Saussy, 16.

9. Grant, 217.

10. Townes, 122.

11. Diana L. Hayes, *Hagar's Daughter: Womanist Ways of Being in the World* (New York: Paulist Press, 1995) 33.

12. Ibid.

13. The dialogue quoted here is from Alice Walker, *The Color Purple* (New York: Harcourt Brace Jovanovich, 1992) 213.

14. Grant, 214.

15. Ibid.

16. Ibid.

17. Letty Russell, *Household of Freedom: Authority in Feminist Theology* (Philadelphia: Westminster Press, 1984) 46.

18. Ibid.

## 3. My Soul Looks Back

1. Vashti M. McKenzie, *Not without a Struggle: Leadership Development for African American Women in Ministry* (Cleveland: United Church Press, 1996) 17–19.

2. E. Franklin Frazier, *The Negro Church in America,* and C. Eric Lincoln, *The Black Church since Frazier* (New York: Schocken Books, 1974) 18.

3. M. Shawn Copeland, "Wading through Many Sorrows," in Emilie M. Townes, ed., *A Troubling in My Soul: Womanist Perspectives on Evil and Suffering* (Maryknoll, N.Y.: Orbis Books, 1993) 113.

4. Paula Giddings, *When and Where I Enter: The Impact of Black Women on Race and Sex in America* (New York: Bantam Books, 1984) 39.

5. Delores S. Williams, *Sisters in the Wilderness: The Challenge of Womanist God-Talk* (Maryknoll, N.Y.: Orbis Books, 1993) 40.

6. Carol Saussy, *God Images and Self-Esteem* (Louisville, Ky.: Westminster/John Knox, 1991) 55.

7. Frances E. Wood, "Take My Yoke upon You," in Townes, 39.

8. Carolyn G. Heilbrun, *Writing a Woman's Life* (New York: Ballentine Books, 1988) 54.

9. bell hooks, *Sisters of the Yam* (Boston: South End Press, 1993) 24.

10. Jacquelyn Grant, "Black Theology and the Black Woman," in Gayraud S. Wilmore and James H. Cone, eds., *Black Theology: A Documentary History, 1966–1979* (Maryknoll, N.Y.: Orbis Books, 1979) 423.

11. Williams, 45.

## 4. Revising Ourselves

1. Christine Renee Robinson, "Black Women: A Tradition of Self-Reliant Strength," *Women Changing Therapy* 5 (Fall 1990): 135–44.

2. Anita P. Jackson and Susan Sears, "Implications of an Afri-centric Worldview in Reducing Stress for African American Women," *Journal of Counseling and Development* 71 (Nov./Dec. 1992): 184–89.

3. Darielle Watts-Jones, "Toward a Stress Scale for African American Women," *Psychology of Women Quarterly* 14 (Fall 1990): 271–75.

4. Ibid.

5. Ibid.

6. Monica McGoldrick and Randy Gerson, *Genograms in Family Assessment* (New York: W. W. Norton, 1985) 1.

7. Ibid., 10.

8. Ibid.

## 5. Sisterhood Future Style

1. bell hooks, *Feminist Theory from Margin to Center* (Boston: South End Press, 1984) 47.

2. Ibid., 43.

3. Ibid., 49.

4. Katie G. Cannon, "Womanist Perspective Discourse and Canon Formation," *Journal of Feminist Studies in Religion* 29 (Fall 1993): 39–47.

## 6. Rocking the Cradle and the World

1. Delores S. Williams, *Sisters in the Wilderness: The Challenge of Womanist God-Talk* (Maryknoll, N.Y.: Orbis Books, 1993) 40.

2. Ibid., 41.

3. Ibid.

4. Ibid.

5. Cheryl J. Sanders, *Living the Intersection: Womanism and Afrocentrism in Theology* (Minneapolis: Fortress Press, 1995) 134.

6. Ibid., 134.

7. Ibid., 135.

8. Ibid.

## 7. Brothers

1. Vashti M. McKenzie, *Not without a Struggle: Leadership Development for African American Women in Ministry* (Cleveland: United Church Press, 1996) 47.

2. Ibid., 49.

3. Ibid., 51.

4. Jean Baker Miller, *Toward a New Psychology for Women* (Boston: Beacon Press, 1976) 6.

5 Ibid.

6. Veronica Chambers, "No More Waiting Our Turn," *Glamour* (September 1995): 144.

7. Emilie M. Townes, ed., *A Troubling in My Soul: Womanist Perspectives on Evil and Suffering* (Maryknoll, N.Y.: Orbis Books, 1993) 42.

8. bell hooks, *Feminist Theory from Margin to Center* (Boston: South End Press, 1984) 74.

9. Ibid., 75.

10. Ibid., 75.

11. Ibid., 72.

12. Ibid., 73.

13. Jane Dempsey Douglass and James F. Kay, eds., *Women, Gender and Christian Community* (Louisville: Westminster John Knox Press, 1997) 14.

14. Ibid.

15. Ibid.

16. Ibid., 18.

## 8. Sins of the Father

1. David Popenoe, *Life without Father* (New York: Martin Kessler Books, 1996) 163.

2. Phyllis Trible, *Texts of Terror: Literary-Feminist Readings of Biblical Narratives* (Overtures to Biblical Theology; Philadelphia: Fortress Press, 1984) 53.

3. Ibid., 104.

4. David Blankenhorn, "The First Man in Every Girl's Life," *Headway* 8 (September 1996): 10.

5. Popenoe, 19.

6. Blankenhorn, 10.

7. Ibid.

8. Ibid.

9. Sheneska Jackson, *Lil Momma's Rules* (New York: Simon and Schuster, 1997) 37.

10. Popenoe, 57.

11. Ibid., 3.

12. Duane F. Reinert and Caroline E. Smith, "Childhood Sexual Abuse and Female Spiritual Development," *Counseling Values* 14 (April 1997): 237.

13. Maxine Glaz and Jeanne Stevenson Moessner, eds. *Women in Travail and Transition* (Minneapolis: Fortress Press, 1991) 110.

14. Pamela Cooper-White, *The Cry of Tamar: Violence against Women and the Church's Response* (Minneapolis: Fortress Press, 1995) 155.

15. Ibid.

16. Marcia Dyson, "Can You Love God and Sex?" *Essence* 28, no. 10 (February 1999): 104.

17. Judith Lewis Herman, *Trauma and Recovery: The Aftermath of Violence from Domestic Abuse to Political Terror* (New York: Harper Collins, 1992) 112.

18. Ibid., 11.

19. Ibid.

20. Cooper-White, 164.

21. Herman, 111.

22. Ibid.

23. Reinert and Smith, 242.

24. Ibid.

25. Linda Hollies, *Taking Back My Yesterdays* (Cleveland: Pilgrim Press, 1997) 3.

## 9. It's Time for Love

1. bell hooks, *Sisters of the Yam* (Boston: South End Press, 1993) 118.

2. Kelly Brown Douglas, "To Reflect the Image of God," in Cheryl J. Sanders, ed., *Living the Intersection: Womanism and Afrocentrism in Theology* (Minneapolis: Fortress Press, 1995) 72.

3. Delores Williams, *Sisters in the Wilderness: The Challenge of Womanist God-Talk* (Maryknoll, N.Y.: Orbis Books, 1993) 73.

4. Bettye Collier-Thomas, *Daughters of Thunder: Black Women Preachers and Their Sermons, 1850–1975* (San Francisco: Jossey-Bass Publishers, 1998) xiv.

5. Renita J. Weems, "The Song of Songs: Introduction, Commentary, and Reflection," *The New Interpreters' Bible* (Nashville: Abingdon Press, 1997) 398.

6. hooks, 75.

7. Harriet G. Lerner, *The Dance of Anger: A Woman's Guide to Changing the Patterns of Intimate Relationships* (New York: Harper and Row, 1985) 20.

8. Carolyn G. Heilbrun, *Writing a Woman's Life* (New York: Ballentine Books, 1988) 87.

9. hooks, 158.

## 10. Becoming One Flesh

1. Harriet G. Lerner, *The Dance of Intimacy: A Woman's Guide to Courageous Acts of Change in Key Relationships* (New York: Harper and Row, 1989) 3.

2. Letty M. Russell and J. Shannon Clarkson, eds., *The Dictionary of Feminist Theologies* (Louisville: Westminster John Knox Press, 1996) 172.

3. Ina Praetorius, *Morality and the Meaning of Life* (Leuven, Belgium: Peeters, 1998) 162.

4. "Most Women Unmarried When First Child Conceived," *The Dallas Morning News* (November 9, 1999): 5A.

5. Stephen A. Grulan, *Marriage and the Family* (Grand Rapids, Mich.: Zondervan Publishers, 1999) 121.

6. Renita Weems, *Battered Love: Marriage, Sex, and Violence in the Hebrew Prophets* (Overtures to Biblical Theology; Minneapolis: Fortress Press, 1995) 26.

7. Ibid., 27.

8. Ibid., 33.

9. Ibid., 42.

10. Russell and Clarkson, 173.

11. Grulan, 123.

12. Ibid., 124.

13. Ibid.

14. Ibid., 125.

15. Ibid., 126.

16. Ibid.

17. Ibid.

## 11. Cleaning Up the House

1. Emilie M. Townes, *In a Blaze of Glory: Womanist Spirituality as a Social Witness* (Nashville: Abingdon Press, 1995) 72.

2. Ibid.

3. Letty M. Russell, *Household of Freedom: Authority in Feminist Theology* (Philadelphia: Westminster Press, 1987), 60.

4. Carol E. Becker, *Leading Women: How Church Women Can Avoid Leadership Traps and Negotiate the Gender Maze* (Nashville: Abingdon Press, 1996) 180.

5. Townes, 73.

6. Ibid.

7. Ibid., 74.

8. Becker, 169.

9. Janet L. Weathers, "Gender and Small Group Communication," in Jane D. Douglass and James F. Kay, eds., *Women, Gender and Christian Community* (Louisville, Ky.: Westminster John Knox Press, 1997) 122.

10. bell hooks, *Sisters of the Yam* (Boston: South End Press, 1993) 169.

11. Jean Baker Miller, *Toward a New Psychology for Women* (Boston: Beacon Press, 1976) 6.

12. Ibid.

13. Carol Pierce and Bill Page, *A Male/Female Continuum: Paths to Colleagueship* (Laconia, N.H.: 1986) 24.

14. Becker, 39.

15. Ibid., 40.

16. Ibid., 41.

17. Ibid., 164.

18. Ibid., 169.

19. Vashti M. McKenzie, *Not without a Struggle: Leadership Development for African American Women in Ministry* (Cleveland: United Church Press, 1996) 84.

20. Ibid., 85.

21. Ibid.

22. Ibid.

23. Sheron C. Patterson, *The Love Clinic: There Is a Doctor in the House* (Dallas: Black Pearl Press, 1999) 15.

24. Becker, 150.

25. Ibid., 151.

26. Ibid.

27. Townes, 39.

28. Ibid., 42.

29. Ibid., 195.

30. Ibid., 42.

31. Weathers, 118.

32. Weathers, 117.

33. McKenzie, 117.

# Suggested Reading

*The following is a list of womanist theologians and some of their recommended works:*

Dr. Renita J. Weems is associate professor of Hebrew Bible at Vanderbilt Divinity School in Nashville, Tennessee. She has written many books, among them *Just a Sister Away: A Womanist View of Women's Relationships in the Bible* (Philadelphia: Innisfree Press, 1991) and *I Asked for Intimacy: Stories of Blessings, Betrayals, and Birthings* (Philadelphia: Innisfree Press, 1993).

Dr. Delores S. Williams is associate professor of theology and culture at Union Theological Seminary in New York. She is the author of *Sisters in the Wilderness: The Challenge of Womanist God-Talk* (Maryknoll, N.Y.: Orbis Books, 1993).

Dr. Jacquelyn Grant is associate professor of systematic theology at the Interdenominational Theological Center in Atlanta. She is the author of *White Women's Christ, Black Women's Jesus: Feminist Christology and Womanist Response* (Atlanta: Scholars Press, 1989).

Dr. Cheryl J. Sanders is associate professor of Christian ethics at Howard University School of Divinity in Washington, D.C. She has written, among others, *Empowerment Ethics for a Liberated People: A Path to African American Social Transformation* (Minneapolis: Fortress Press, 1995).

Dr. Emilie M. Townes is professor of Christian Ethics at Union Theological Seminary in New York City. One of her books is *A Troubling in My Soul: Womanist Perspectives on Evil and Suffering* (Maryknoll, N.Y.: Orbis Books, 1993).